SRA

Early Interventions in Reading

Story-Time Readers Blackline Masters

Columbus, OH

The McGraw-Hill Companies

MHEonline.com

SRA

Imprint 2012

Send all inquiries to:
SRA/McGraw-Hill
8787 Orion Place
Columbus, OH 43240-4027

Printed in the United States of America.

ISBN 0-07-603651-0

7 8 9 DOH 13

Table of Contents

About the Blackline Masters

The ***SRA Early Interventions in Reading*** *Story-Time Readers Blackline Masters* allow your students to apply their knowledge of phonic elements to read simple, engaging texts. Each story supports instruction in a new phonic element and incorporates elements and words that have been learned earlier.

The students can fold and staple the pages of each story to make books of their own to keep and read. We suggest that you keep extra sets of the stories in your classroom for the children to reread.

How to fold a blackline master story

1. Tear out the pages you need.

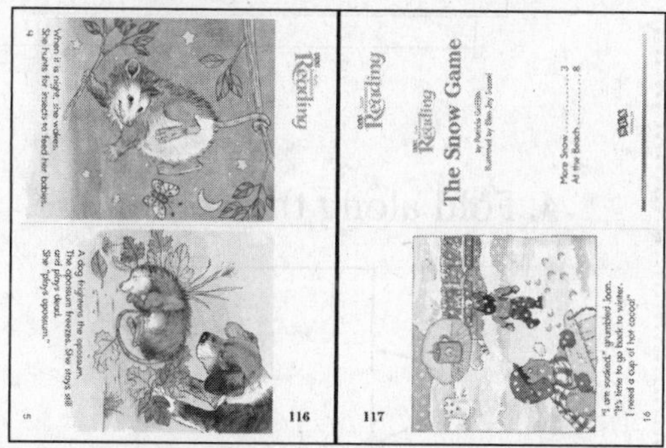

2. For 16-page stories, place pages 8 and 9, 6 and 11, 4 and 13, and 2 and 15 faceup.

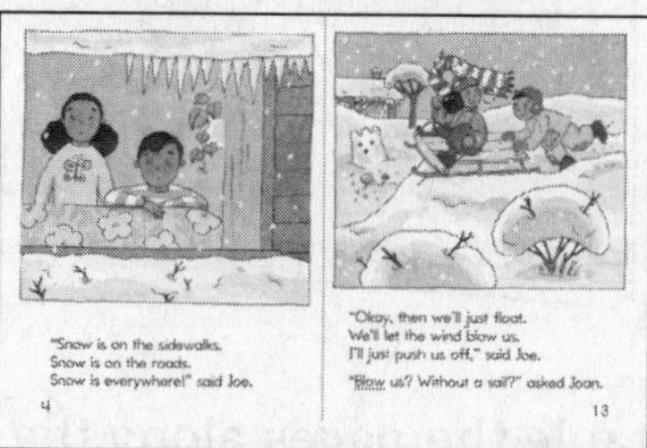

2. For 8-page stories, place pages 4 and 5 and pages 2 and 7 faceup.

For 16-page book

3. Place the pages on top of each other in this order: pages 8 and 9, pages 6 and 11, pages 4 and 13, and pages 2 and 15.

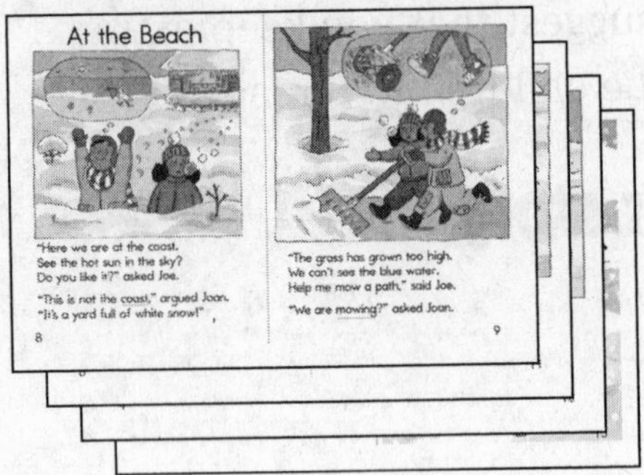

4. Fold along the center line.

5. Check to make sure the pages are in order.

6. Staple the pages along the fold.

For 8-page book

3. Place pages 4 and 5 on top of pages 2 and 7.

4. Fold along the center line.

5. Check to make sure the pages are in order.

6. Staple the pages along the fold.

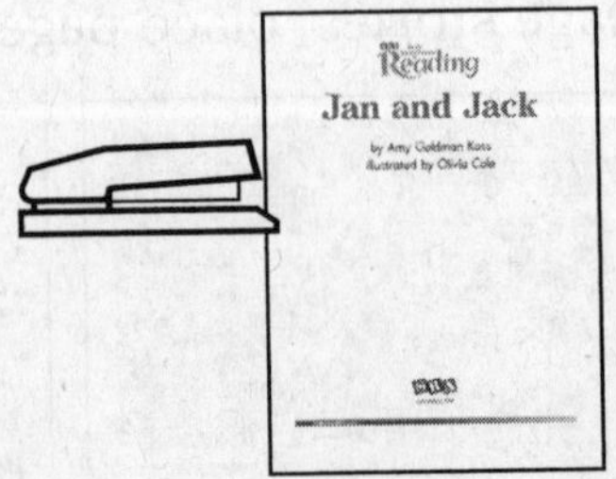

Just to let you know...

A message from ______________________________

Help your child discover the joy of independent reading with ***SRA Early Interventions in Reading***. From time to time your child will bring home his or her very own story to share with you. With your help, these stories can give your child important reading practice and a joyful shared reading experience.

You may want to set aside a few minutes every evening to read these stories together. Here are some suggestions you may find helpful:

- Do not expect your child to read each story perfectly, but concentrate on sharing the book together.
- Participate by doing some of the reading.
- Talk about the stories as you read, give lots of encouragement, and watch as your child becomes more fluent throughout the year!

Learning to read takes lots of practice. Sharing these stories is one way that your child can gain that valuable practice. Encourage your child to keep the stories in a special place. This collection will make a library of books that your child can read and reread. Take the time to listen to your child read from his or her library. Just a few moments of shared reading each day can give your child the confidence needed to excel in reading.

Children who read every day come to think of reading as a pleasant, natural part of life. One way to inspire your child to read is to show that reading is an important part of your life by letting him or her see you reading books, magazines, newspapers, or any other materials. Another good way to show that you value reading is to share one of these stories with your child each day.

Successful reading experiences allow children to be proud of their newfound reading ability. Support your child with interest and enthusiasm about reading. You won't regret it!

Para su conocimiento...

Un mensaje de ____

Ayude a su niño o niña a descubrir el placer de la lectura individual con ***SRA Early Interventions in Reading***. De vez en cuando, su niño(a) llevará a casa su propio cuento para compartirlo con usted. Con su ayuda, estos cuentos pueden constituir un ejercicio importante para mejorar la lectura y una experiencia placentera de lectura compartida.

Disponga de unos minutos en las noches para leer estos cuentos con su niño(a). Estas sugerencias lo pueden ayudar:

- No espere que lea el cuento a la perfección, concéntrese sólo en leer el libro juntos.
- Participe leyendo fragmentos del cuento.
- Conforme lean, comente con su niño(a) los cuentos, aliéntelo constantemente y observe cómo mejora su fluidez durante el año.

Aprender a leer requiere mucha práctica. Compartir estos cuentos es una forma de ayudar a su niño(a) a adquirir esa valiosa destreza. Anímelo a guardar los cuentos en un lugar especial. Esta colección constituirá una biblioteca que el niño podrá leer y releer. Dedique tiempo a escuchar a su niño(a) cuando lea los libros de su biblioteca. Tan sólo unos momentos de lectura compartida todos los días le darán a su niño(a) la confianza necesaria para convertirse en un excelente lector.

Los niños que leen todos los días llegan a hacer de la lectura una parte placentera y natural de la vida. Una forma de inspirar a su niño(a) a leer es demostrarle que la lectura es un aspecto importante para usted; propicie que lo vea leer libros, revistas, periódicos y otras publicaciones. Otra buena manera de demostrarle que usted valora la lectura es compartiendo con él(ella) uno de estos cuentos todos los días.

Las experiencias exitosas con la lectura hacen que los niños se sientan orgullosos de su recién adquirida habilidad para leer. Apoye a su niño(a) demostrando interés y entusiasmo en la lectura. ¡No se arrepentirá!

1

The socks are on the feet!

Have child read this book to you, sign here, and return ____________________

The Baby

by Amy Goldman Koss
illustrated by Sylvie Wickstrom

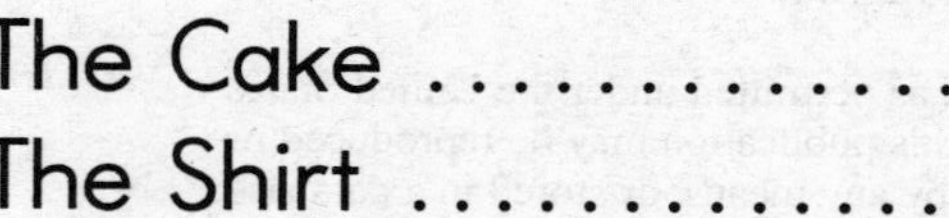

Columbus, OH
The McGraw-Hill Companies

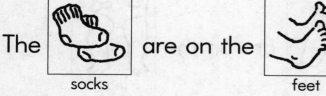

MHEonline.com

McGraw Hill SRA

Imprint 2012

Printed in the United States of America.

Send all inquiries to:
SRA/McGraw-Hill
8787 Orion Place
Columbus, OH 43240-4027

The McGraw-Hill Companies

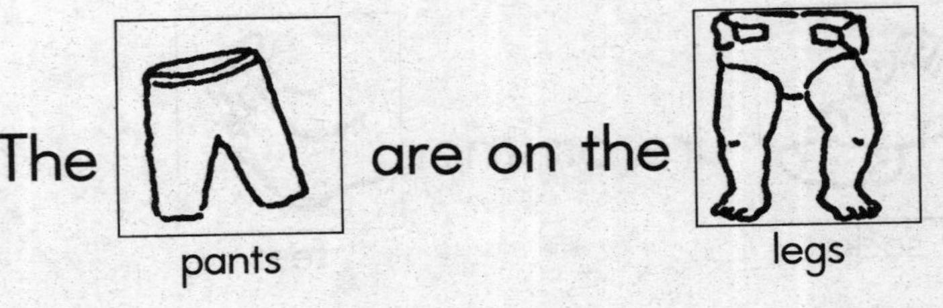

The pants are on the legs.

3

The  is on the 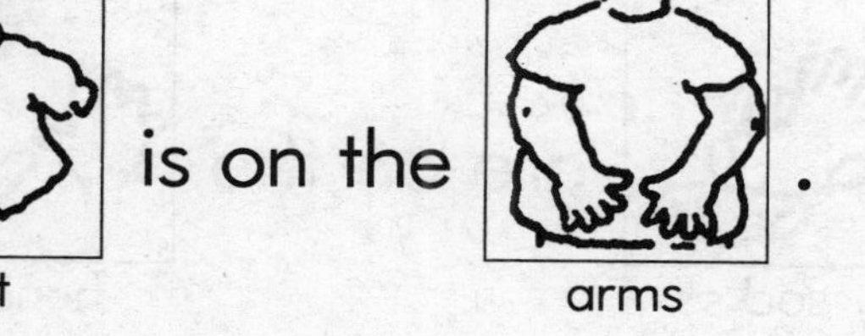 .

shirt arms

The Cake

The  is in the chair.

baby

The [cake] is on the [ear].

The  [socks] are on the [hands].

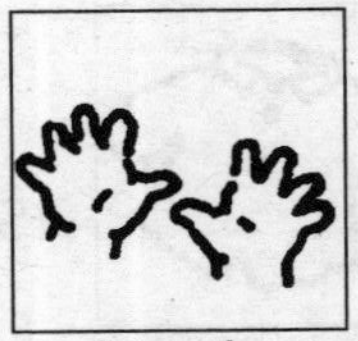

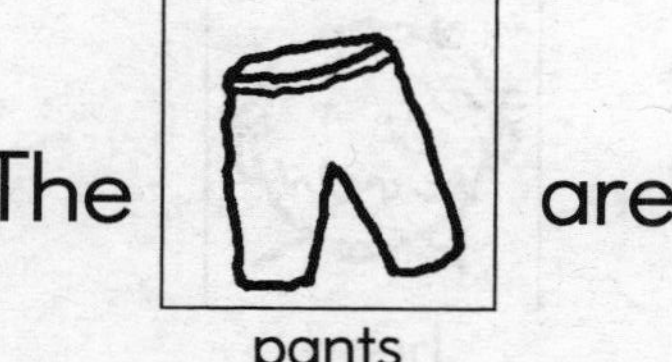

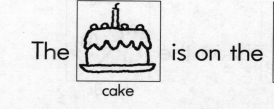

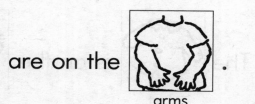

The pants are on the arms.

The cake is on the nose.

cake
nose

The [cake] is on the [hands] .

The Shirt

The [shirt] is on the [head] .

7

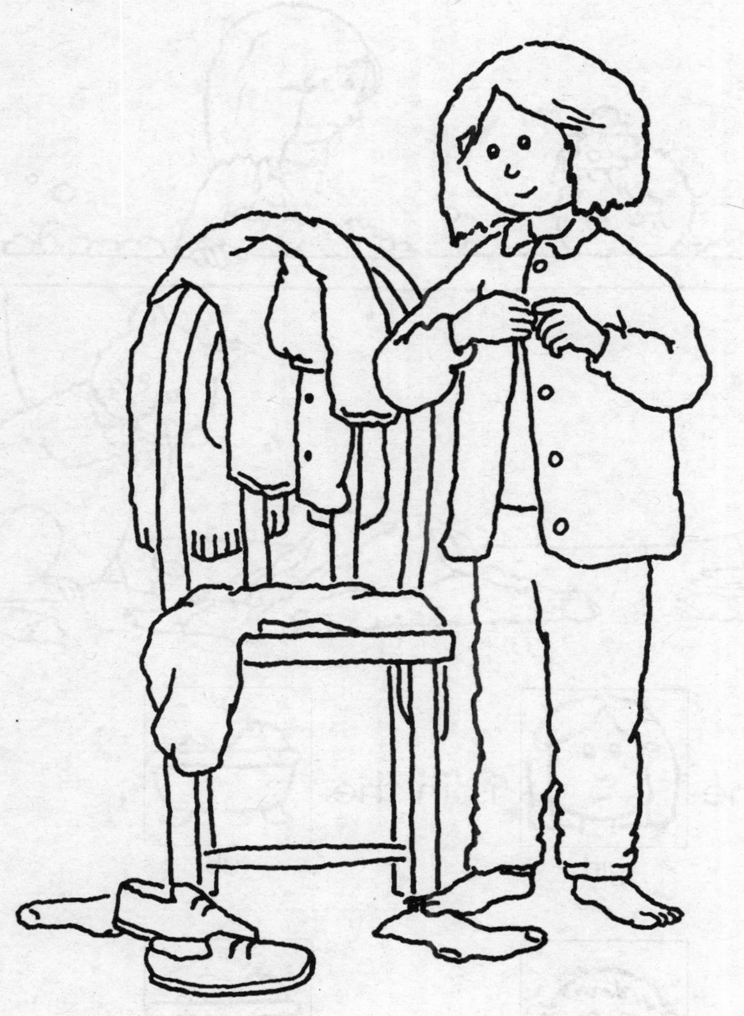

The cake is on the girl.

cake girl

The girl is in the tub.

girl tub

The baby is in the tub.

baby tub

A  .

table

Have child read this book to you, sign here, and return ______________

A Table

by Amy Goldman Koss
illustrated by Yvette Banek

MHEonline.com

SRA

Imprint 2012

Printed in the United States of America.

Send all inquiries to:
SRA/McGraw-Hill
8787 Orion Place
Columbus, OH 43240-4027

Columbus, OH

The McGraw·Hill Companies

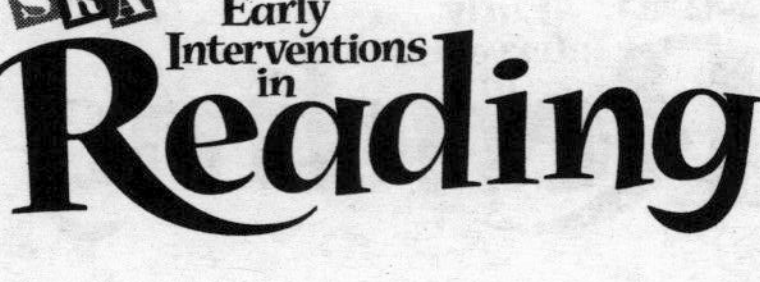
SRA
Early Interventions in
Reading

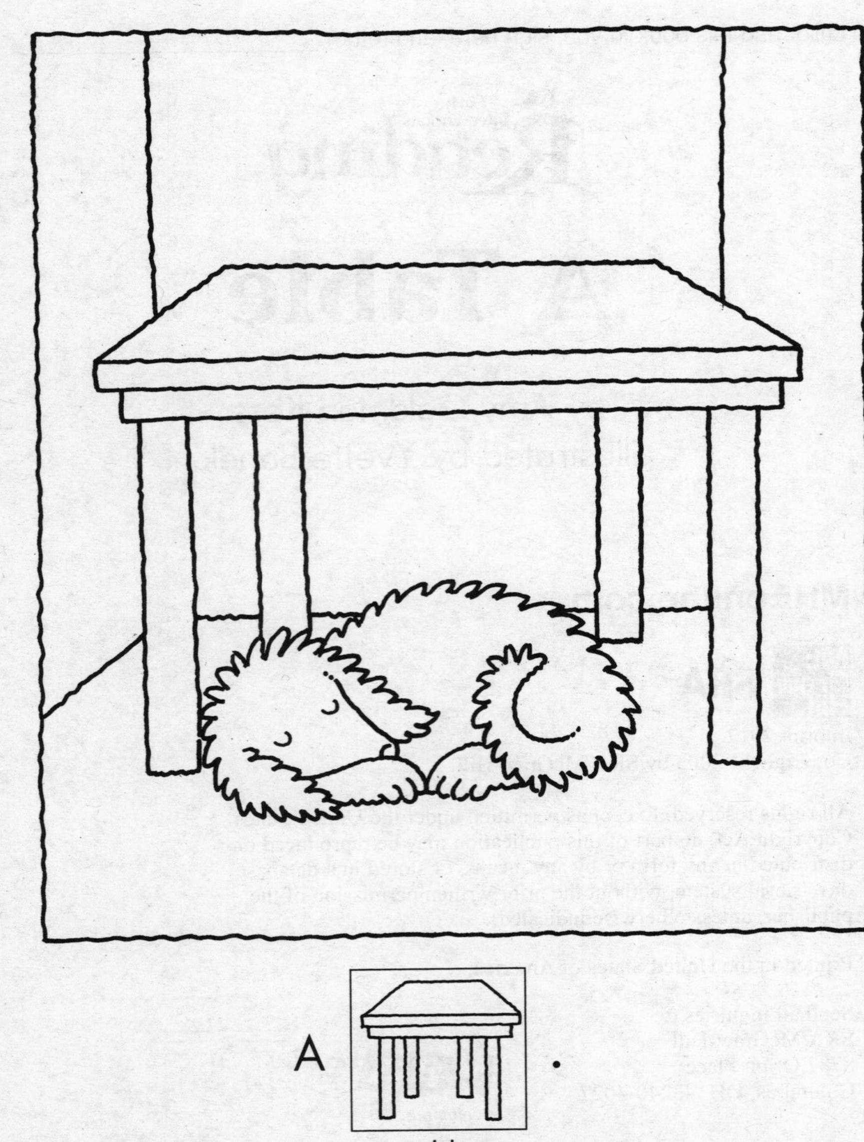

A table.

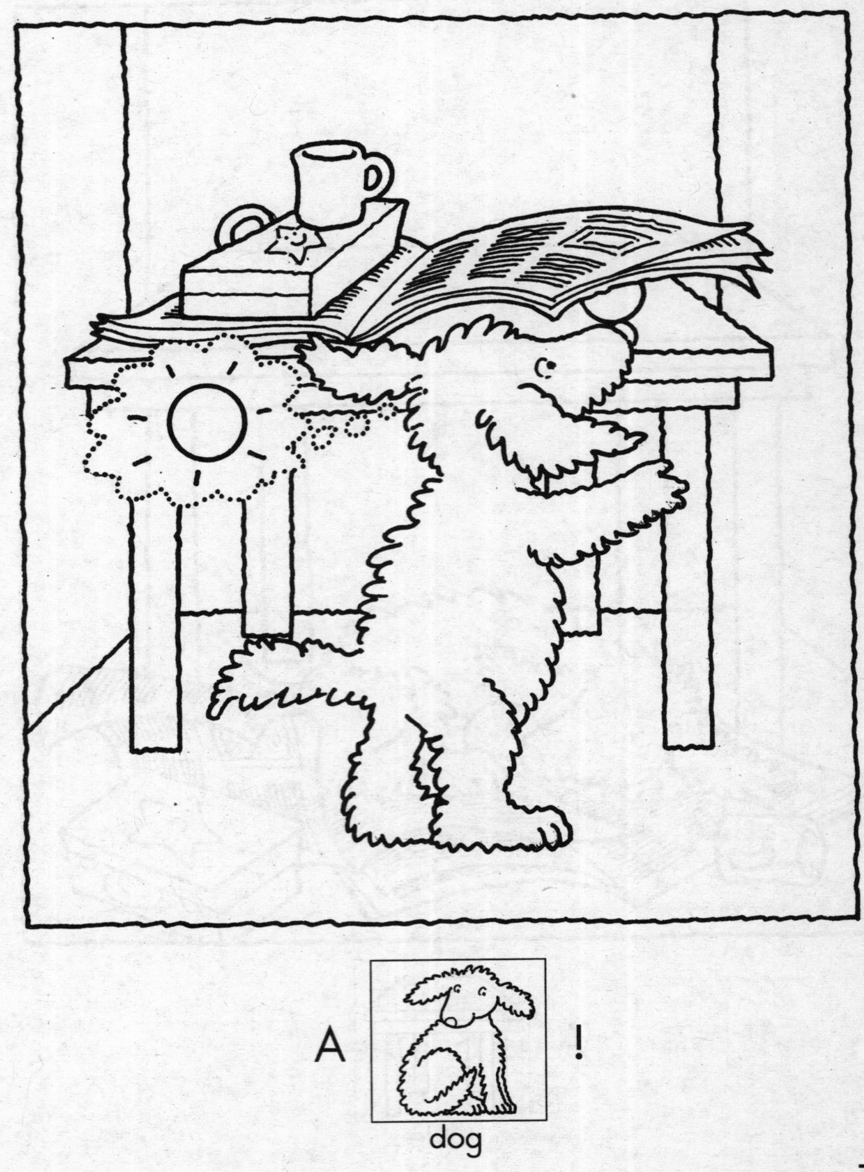

A dog!

A  is on the   .

mug lunch box

A is on the .

ball table

A  newspaper is on the 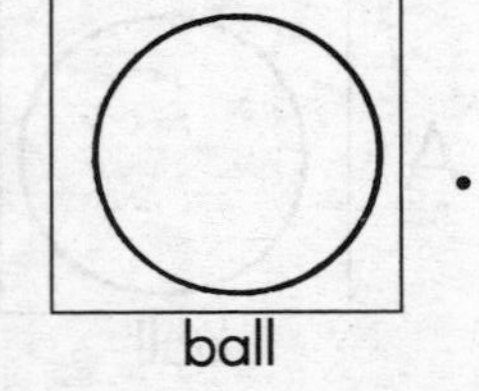 ball.

A  lunch box is on the  newspaper.

In the [egg] WAS a [bird] .

egg

bird

Have child read this book to you, sign here, and return ____________

The Egg

by Amy Goldman Koss
illustrated by Eva Cockerille

MHEonline.com

SRA

Imprint 2012

Printed in the United States of America.

Send all inquiries to:
SRA/McGraw-Hill
8787 Orion Place
Columbus, OH 43240-4027

SRA
Columbus, OH

The McGraw-Hill Companies

On an island is a forest.

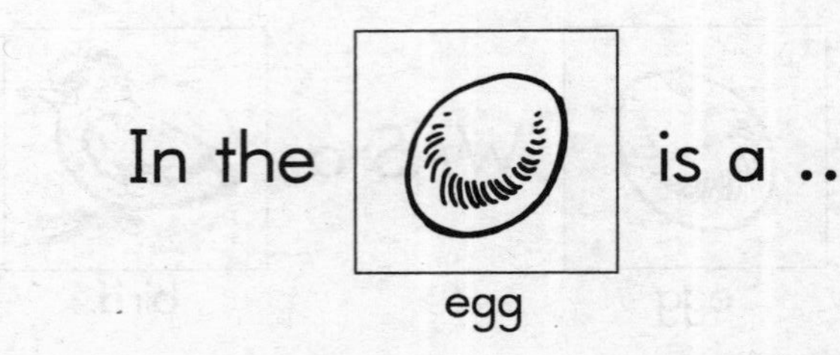

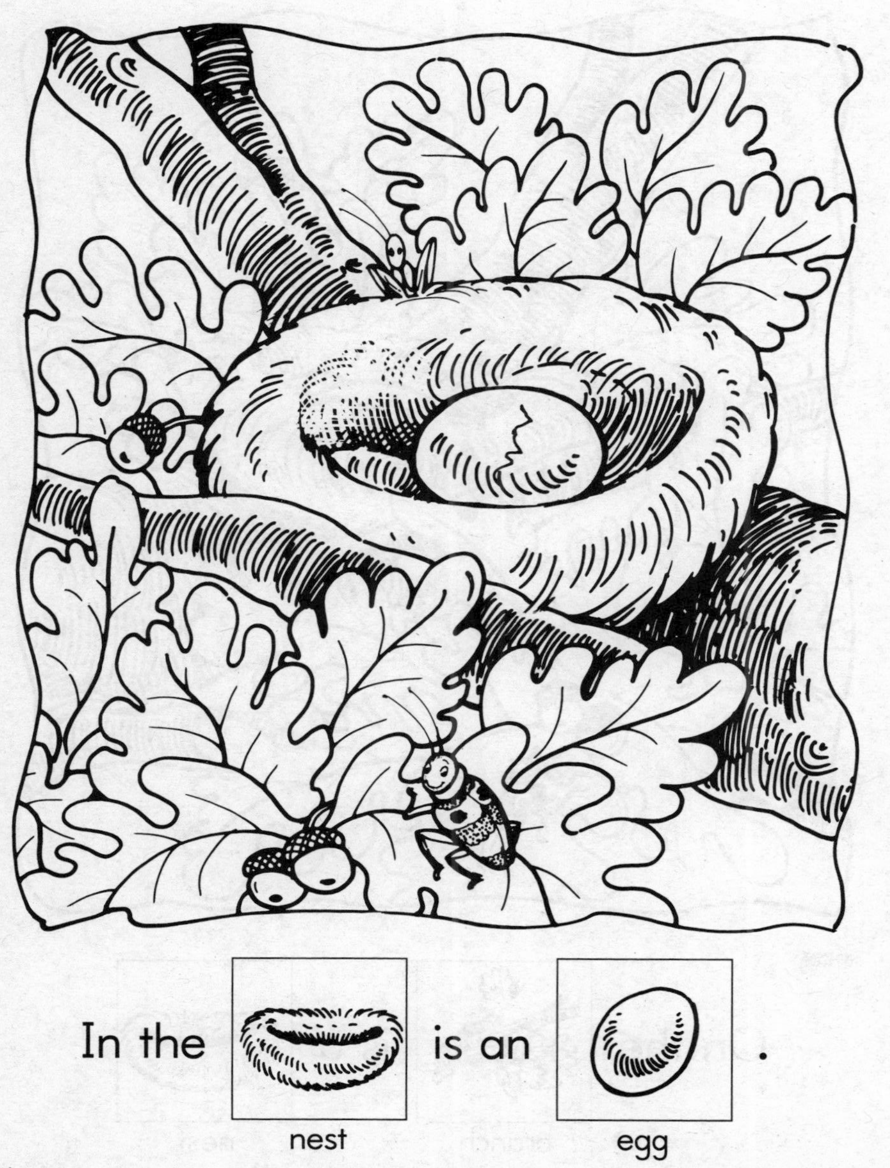

In the [nest] is an [egg].

In the [forest] is a [tree].

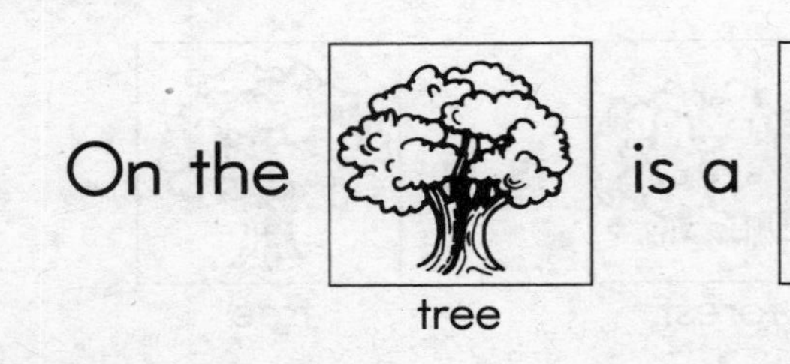

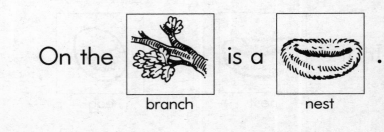

On the [tree] is a [branch].

On the [branch] is a [nest].

A ham!

Have child read this book to you, sign here, and return ____________________

SRA Early Interventions in Reading

The Hat

by Amy Goldman Koss
illustrated by Susanne DeMarco

SRA
Columbus, OH

The McGraw-Hill Companies

MHEonline.com

McGraw-Hill SRA

Imprint 2012

Printed in the United States of America.

Send all inquiries to:
SRA/McGraw-Hill
8787 Orion Place
Columbus, OH 43240-4027

The McGraw-Hill Companies

In the hat is a ham.

Matt.
Matt has a hat.

In the hat is a  rabbit .

In the hat is a  bird .

I can!

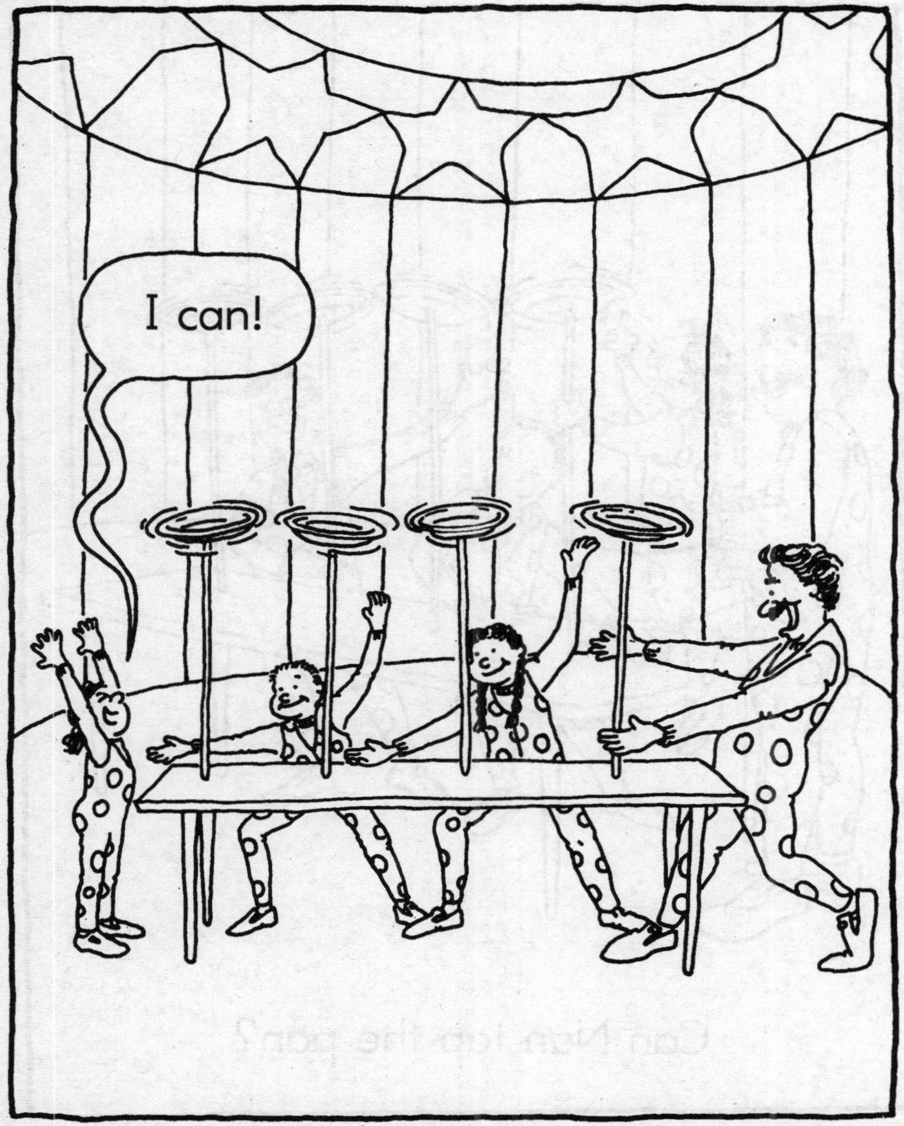

Have child read this book to you, sign here, and return ____________________

Nan's Family

by Anne and Robert O'Brien
illustrated by Linda Kelen

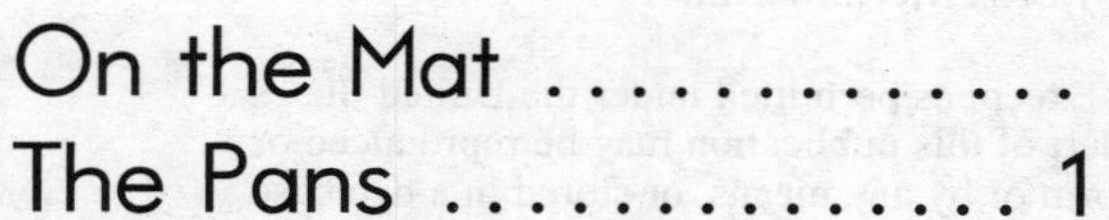

Columbus, OH
The McGraw-Hill Companies

MHEonline.com

Mc Graw Hill SRA

Imprint 2012

Printed in the United States of America.

Send all inquiries to:
SRA/McGraw-Hill
8787 Orion Place
Columbus, OH 43240-4027

The McGraw-Hill Companies

Can Nan tap the pan?

Nan is sad.

On the Mat

Dad sat on the mat.

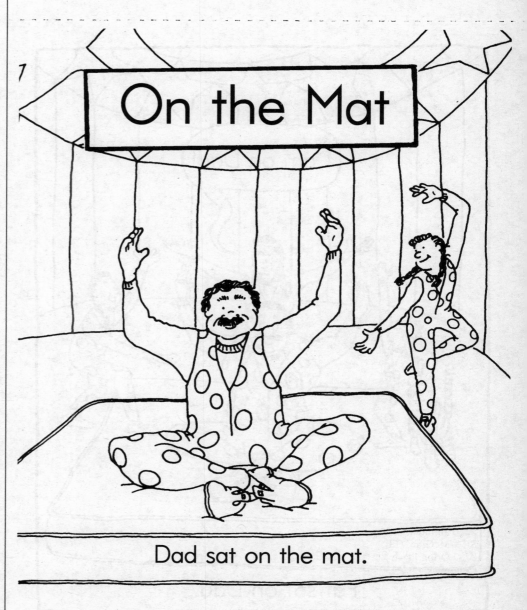

I am on Dad!

Pat sat on Dad.

Dan taps the pan.

Pat taps the pan.

Dan sat on Pat.

SRA
Early Interventions in Reading

I am on Dan and Pat and Dad!

Nan sat on Dan.

The Pans

Dad has a pan.
Dad taps the pan.

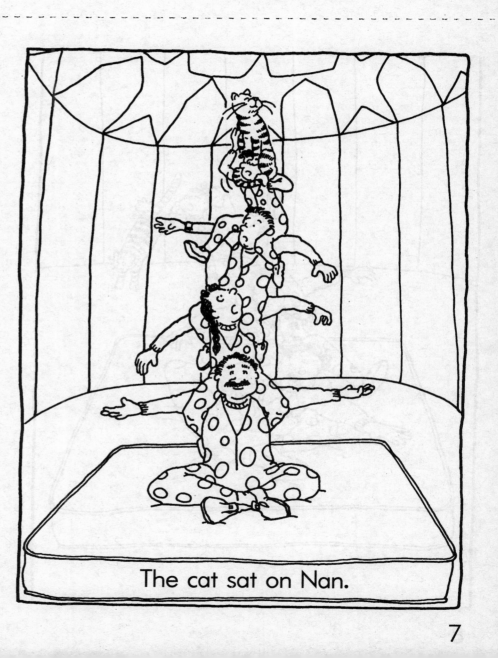

The cat sat on Nan.

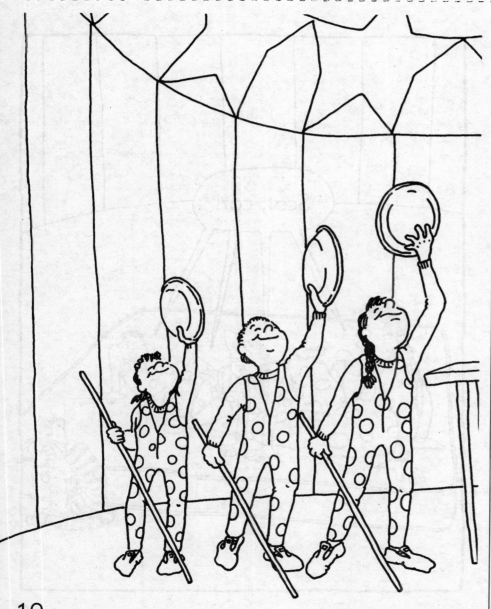

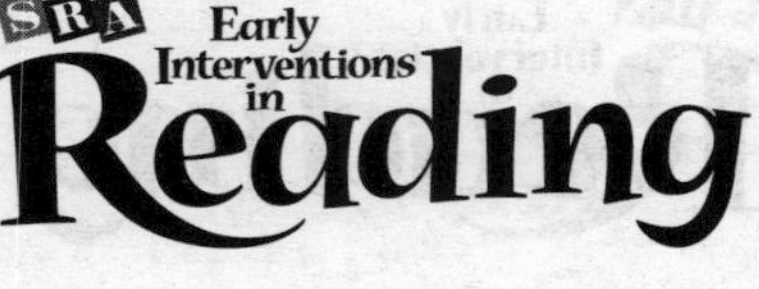
SRA
Early Interventions in
Reading

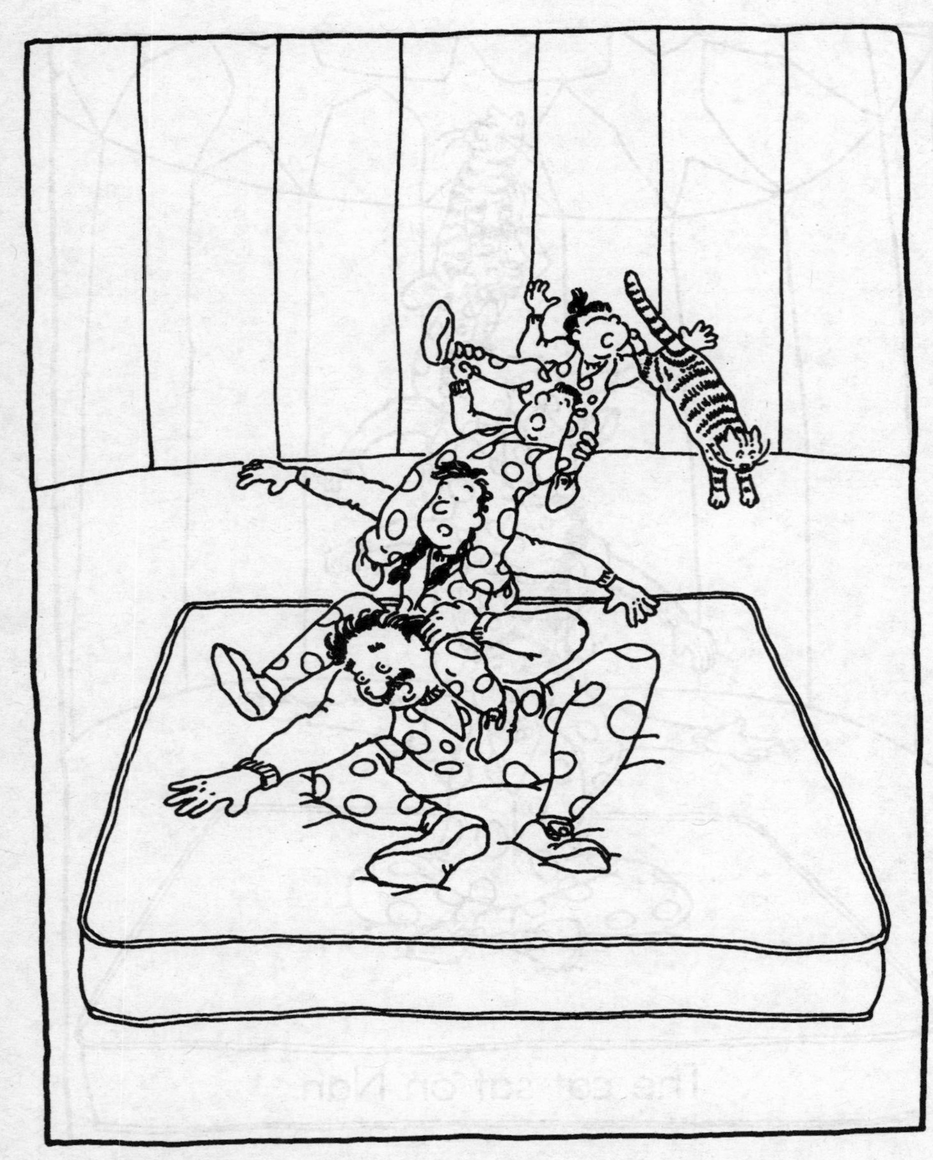

Scat, cat!

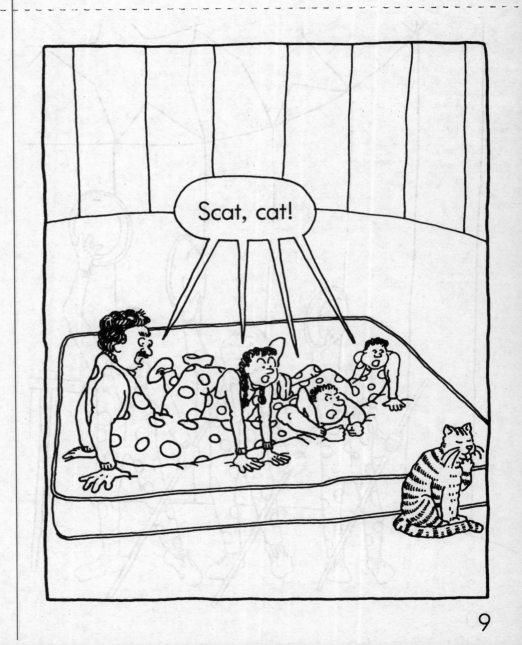

Have child read this book to you, sign here, and return ____________

Pam and the Man

by Dottie Raymer
illustrated by Kate Flanagan

MHEonline.com

SRA

Imprint 2012

Printed in the United States of America.

Send all inquiries to:
SRA/McGraw-Hill
8787 Orion Place
Columbus, OH 43240-4027

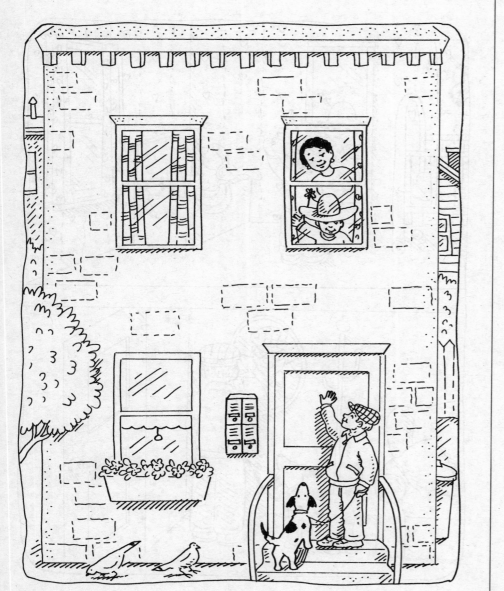

Columbus, OH

The McGraw-Hill Companies

Tap! Tap! Tap!

Tap! Tap! Tap!

Pam has a hat.

The man has a hat.

Pam has a nap.

The man has a nap.

Have child read this book to you, sign here, and return ____________

The Cat

by Amy Goldman Koss
illustrated by Yvette Banek

Columbus, OH

The McGraw-Hill Companies

SRA Early Interventions in Reading

MHEonline.com

Mc Graw Hill SRA

Imprint 2012

Printed in the United States of America.

Send all inquiries to:
SRA/McGraw-Hill
8787 Orion Place
Columbus, OH 43240-4027

The McGraw-Hill Companies

The cat had a nap in a cap!

The cat had a nap on a mat.

The cat had a nap on a pad.

The cat had a nap in a pan.

Have child read this book to you, sign here, and return ______________________

The Tin Man

by Amy Goldman Koss
illustrated by Tony Caldwell

Columbus, OH

The McGraw-Hill Companies

MHEonline.com

McGraw-Hill SRA

Imprint 2012

Printed in the United States of America.

Send all inquiries to:
SRA/McGraw-Hill
8787 Orion Place
Columbus, OH 43240-4027

The McGraw-Hill Companies

Sid has a tin pan.
Sid has a tin can.
Sid has a tin rim.
Sid has a tin man!

SRA Early Interventions in Reading

I am Sid.
I have a tin pan.

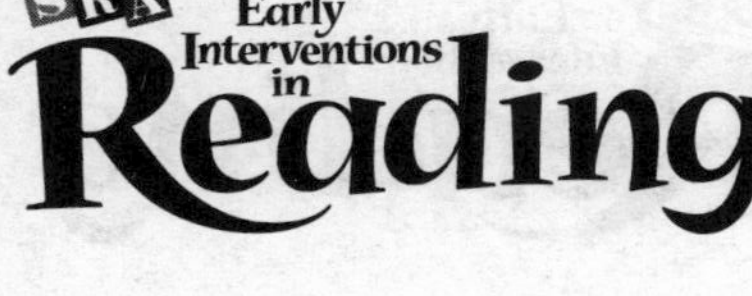

I am Sid.
I have a tin can.

I am Sid.
I have a tin rim.

Have child read this book to you, sign here, and return ____________________

Tim Spins

by Anne O'Brien
illustrated by Steve Henry

Columbus, OH

The McGraw·Hill Companies

MHEonline.com

Mc Graw Hill SRA

Imprint 2012

Printed in the United States of America.

Send all inquiries to:
SRA/McGraw-Hill
8787 Orion Place
Columbus, OH 43240-4027

The McGraw-Hill Companies

Tim hits a pit . . .
and sits.

Tim spins.

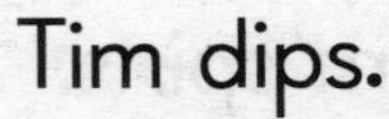
Tim dips.

Tim tips his hat.

Nat is at bat!
NAT

Have child read this book to you, sign here, and return ______________________

SRA Early Interventions in Reading

Nat the Crab

by Alice Cary
illustrated by Doug Cushman

Columbus, OH

The McGraw-Hill Companies

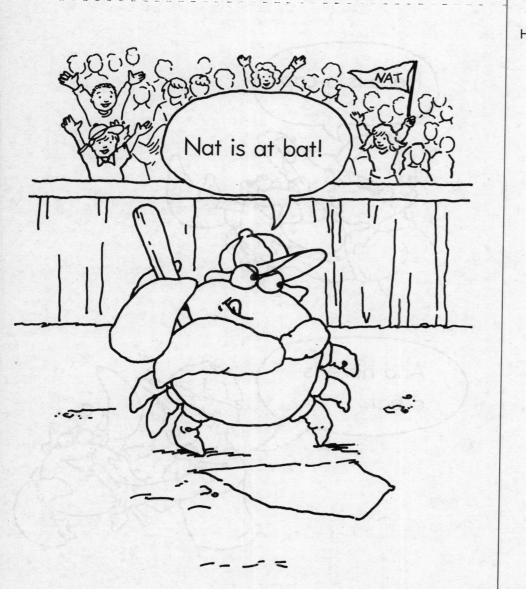

MHEonline.com

McGraw Hill SRA

Imprint 2012

Printed in the United States of America.

Send all inquiries to:
SRA/McGraw-Hill
8787 Orion Place
Columbus, OH 43240-4027

The McGraw-Hill Companies

Here it is, Nat!

Nat's Nap

Nap, Nat!
In the crib, Nat!

A crab can't nap!

A trip in a cab, Nat?
I have the map!

TAXI

A trip, Nat?

A trip! A trip!

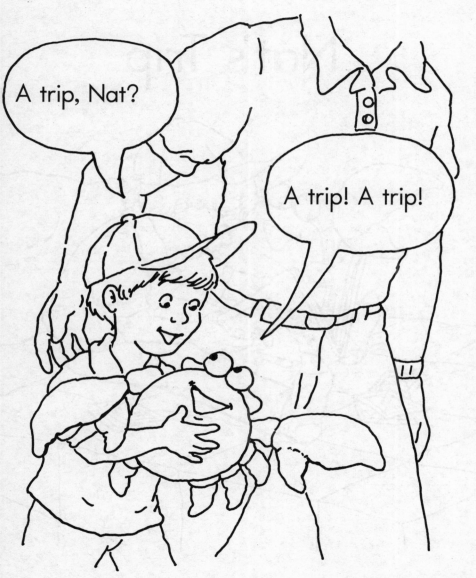

SRA
Early Interventions in Reading

A crab can tap!
A crab can snap!

Nat's Trip

Baseball

SRA
Early Interventions in Reading

A crab can spin
and spin!

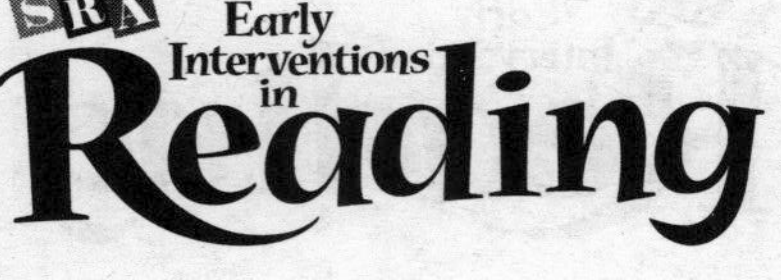
SRA
Early Interventions in
Reading

A crab can sit a bit.

NAT

Nat naps!

Have child read this book to you, sign here, and return ______________

Brad's Ram

by Amy Goldman Koss
illustrated by Yuri Salzman

Columbus, OH

The McGraw-Hill Companies

MHEonline.com

Imprint 2012

Printed in the United States of America.

Send all inquiries to:
SRA/McGraw-Hill
8787 Orion Place
Columbus, OH 43240-4027

The McGraw-Hill Companies

Brad is a trim man.
He has a fat ram.
The ram has a fat hat!

Brad is a trim man.
He has a trim hat.
He has a fat ram.

Brad's ram spins
and nabs the hat.
Brad is mad.
He nabs the hat.

Snap! The hat!

I can sit with Sis and Dad.

Have child read this book to you, sign here, and return ____________________

Sis the Cat

by Mike Dennison
illustrated by Susanne DeMarco

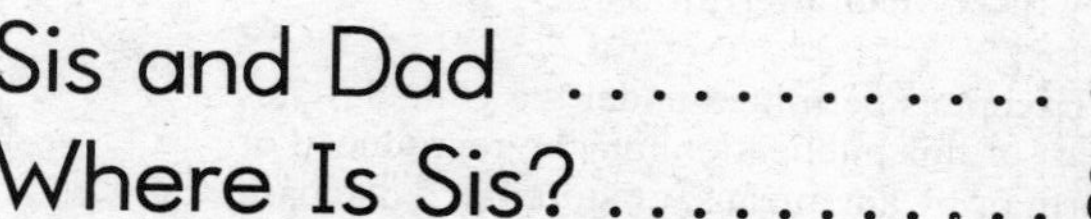

Columbus, OH

The McGraw-Hill Companies

MHEonline.com

SRA

Imprint 2012

Printed in the United States of America.

Send all inquiries to:
SRA/McGraw-Hill
8787 Orion Place
Columbus, OH 43240-4027

The McGraw-Hill Companies

Dad is not mad.
And Sis is not sad.

Dad has Sis.
Sis sits on him.

Sis and Dad

There is Sis. Sis spins and stops on the mat.

Sis can sit.
Sis can nap.

I miss Sis.
Where is Sis?

Is Sis with Sam and Pam?
No, Sis is not with Sam and Pam.

Sis can hit.
Sis can tap.

Sis taps the pans.
Sis hits the hats.

Is Sis in a tin pan?
Sis is not in a tin pan.

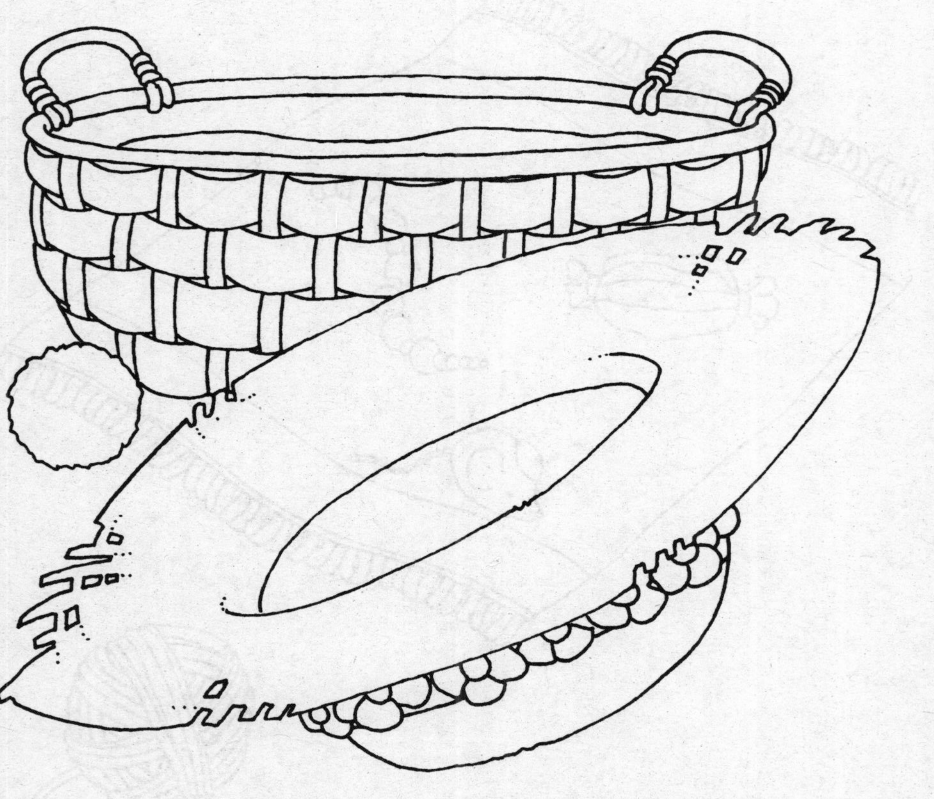

Is Sis in the hat?
Sis is not in the hat.

Dad is mad.
Scat, cat!

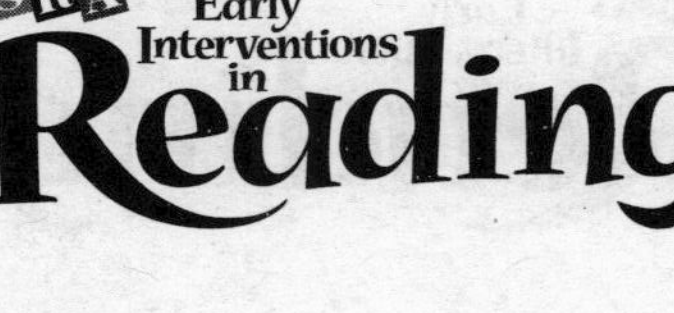

Where Is Sis?

Sis scats.
Where is Sis?

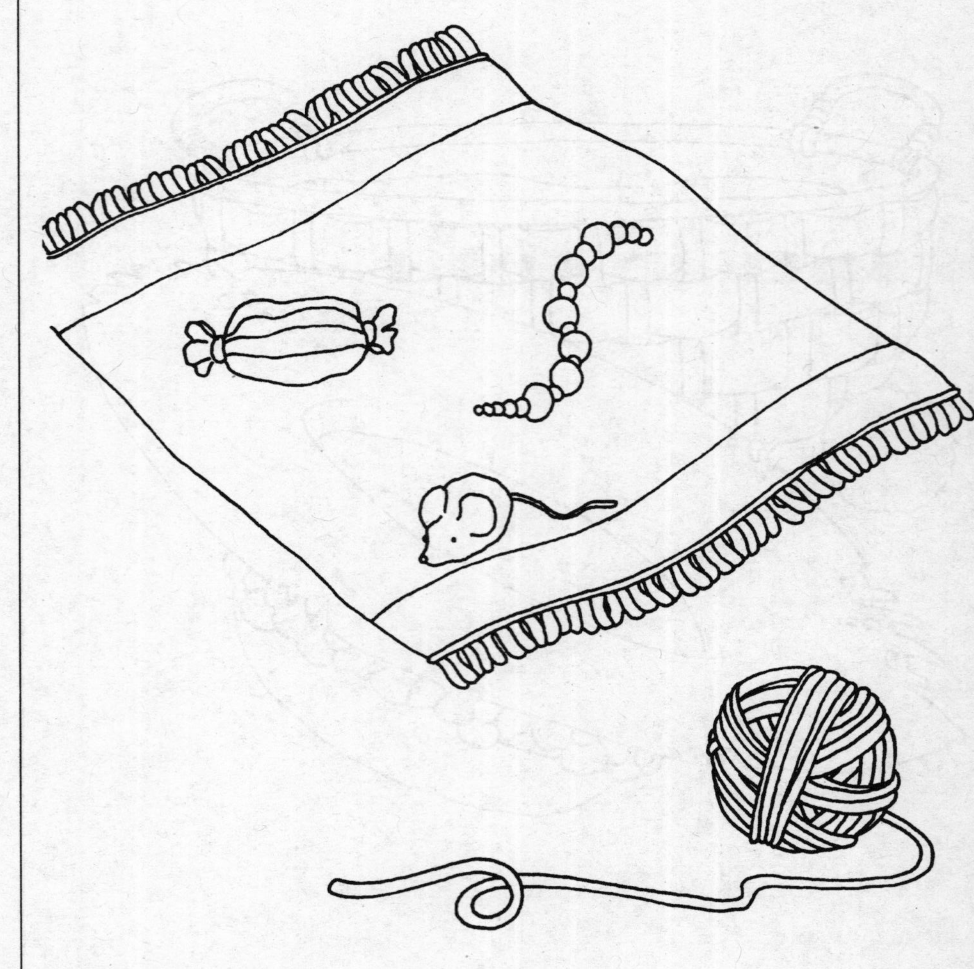

Is Sis on the mat?
Sis is not on the mat.

Yes, a frog can beg.
Yes, a dog can hop.

Have child read this book to you, sign here, and return ______________________

A Frog and a Dog

by Dennis Fertig
illustrated by Loretta Lustig

MHEonline.com

SRA

Imprint 2012

Printed in the United States of America.

Send all inquiries to:
SRA/McGraw-Hill
8787 Orion Place
Columbus, OH 43240-4027

SRA
Columbus, OH

The McGraw·Hill Companies

This is Ted.
Ted is a frog.

Can a frog beg?
Can a dog hop?

Ted the frog can sit on a cot.
Meg the dog can sit on a cot.

This is Meg.
Meg is a dog.

A frog can hop.
A dog can beg.

OOPS!
A frog can hop far.

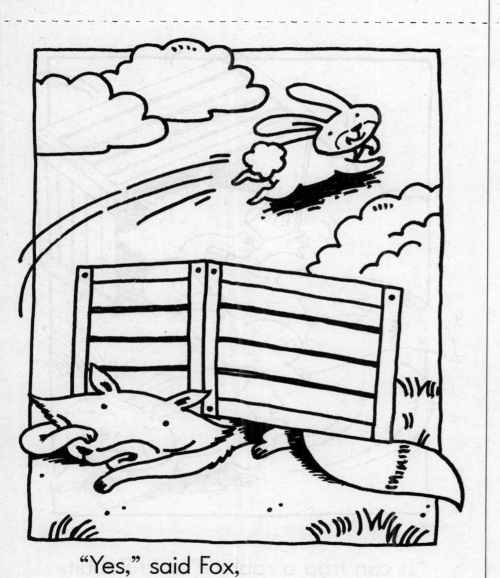

"Yes," said Fox,
"but it did not trap you!"

Have child read this book to you, sign here, and return ______________

A Fox and His Box

by Marj Milano
illustrated by Rusty Fletcher

MHEonline.com

Mc Graw Hill SRA

Imprint 2012

Printed in the United States of America.

Send all inquiries to:
SRA/McGraw-Hill
8787 Orion Place
Columbus, OH 43240-4027

SRA
Columbus, OH

The McGraw-Hill Companies

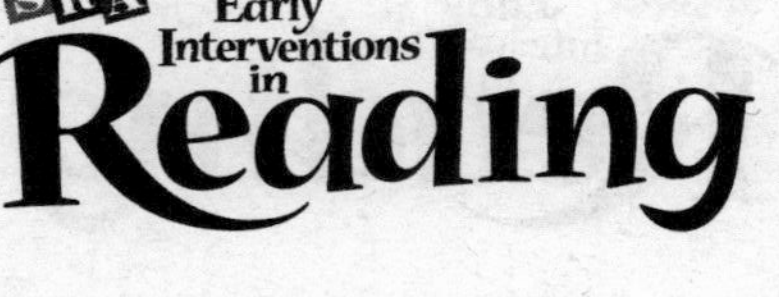

Rabbit and Fox sat on a big box.
"You have a big box," said Rabbit.
"Yes," said Fox. "It is a trap."

"It can trap a rabbit?" said Rabbit.
"But I am a rabbit!"

"Can it trap an ox?" said Rabbit.
"Not an ox," said Fox,
"but it can trap a rabbit."

"Can it trap a frog?" said Rabbit.
"Yes," said Fox. "It can trap a frog."

“Can it trap a cat?” said Rabbit.
“Yes,” said Fox. “It can trap a cat.”

“Can it trap a hog?” said Rabbit.
“Yes,” said Fox. “It can trap a hog.”

"Sinbad, you have bad habits!" says Anna.

Have child read this book to you, sign here, and return ____________________

Sinbad the Pig

by Anne and Robert O'Brien
illustrated by Meg McLean

SRA
Columbus, OH

The McGraw-Hill Companies

MHEonline.com

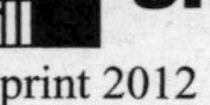

SRA

Imprint 2012

Printed in the United States of America.

Send all inquiries to:
SRA/McGraw-Hill
8787 Orion Place
Columbus, OH 43240-4027

The McGraw-Hill Companies

Anna stamps.
Gramps grins.

Anna trips on the pig.

Sinbad Acts Fast

Gramps and Anna have a big pig.

Sinbad sits.

"I have him!" says Anna.

The pig is Sinbad.
Sinbad has bad habits.

Sinbad tips Gramps.

Anna grabs at Sinbad.
Gramps grins.

Sinbad is fast.
He spins past Anna.

Gramps grabs at Sinbad.
Sinbad acts fast!

Sinbad and Anna

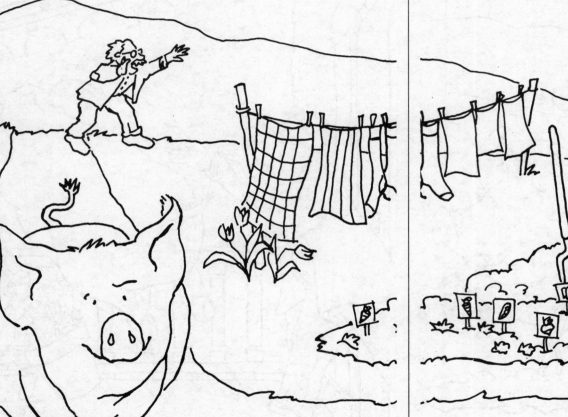

"Grab the pig, Anna!" says Gramps.

Have child read this book to you, sign here, and return ______________________

“I have a star!” said Max.
“Mom, you are smart!”

Grab a Star

by Dottie Raymer
illustrated by Jennifer Emery

MHEonline.com

SRA

Imprint 2012

Printed in the United States of America.

Send all inquiries to:
SRA/McGraw-Hill
8787 Orion Place
Columbus, OH 43240-4027

SRA
Columbus, OH

The McGraw-Hill Companies

"Mom, are stars far away?"
"Yes, Max," said Mom.
"Stars are far, far away."

"Here, Max," said Mom.
"Here is a star for you."

"Mom, can I have a star?"

"Hmm . . . a star . . . ," said Mom.

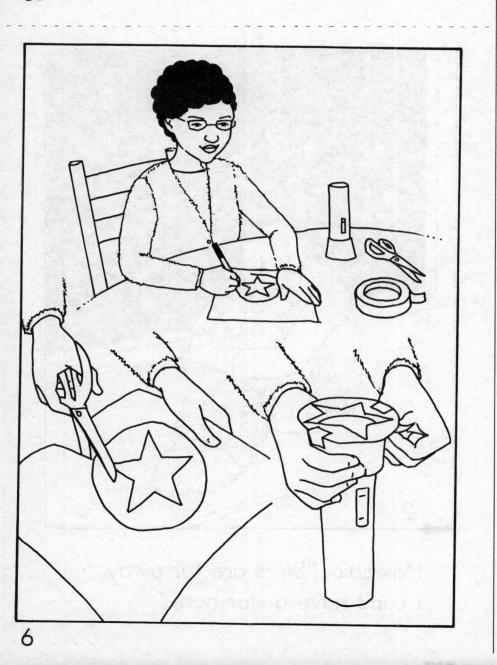

"You sit here, Max," said Mom.
"You can have a star here."

Max said, "Stars are far away.
I can't have a star here."

Amanda Panda has a sax,
and a band,
and tons of fans.
"You are tops!" says Mom.
"Yes, you are tops!" says Pop.

Have child read this book to you, sign here, and return ____________________

Panda Band

by Alice Cary
illustrated by Roz Schanzer

Columbus, OH

The McGraw-Hill Companies

MHEonline.com

SRA

Imprint 2012

Printed in the United States of America.

Send all inquiries to:
SRA/McGraw-Hill
8787 Orion Place
Columbus, OH 43240-4027

The McGraw-Hill Companies

Mac and Max drop in.
"I can have a band!" says Amanda.

"Oh no!" says Mom.
"Oh no!" says Pop.

"Oh no!" says Mom.

"Oh no!" says Pop.

Amanda's Sax

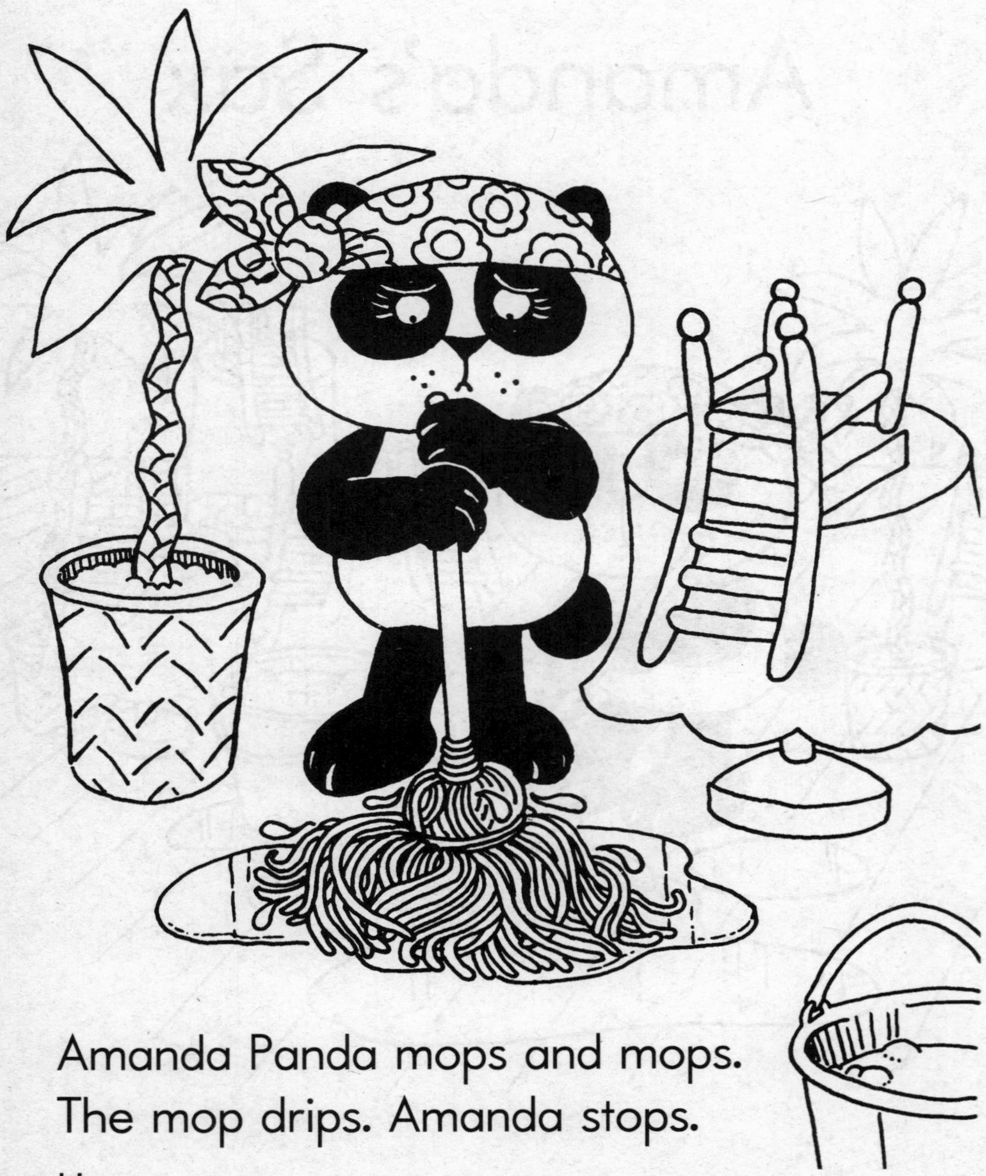

Amanda Panda mops and mops.
The mop drips. Amanda stops.

Amanda's Band

"I can't stand this," Amanda sobs.

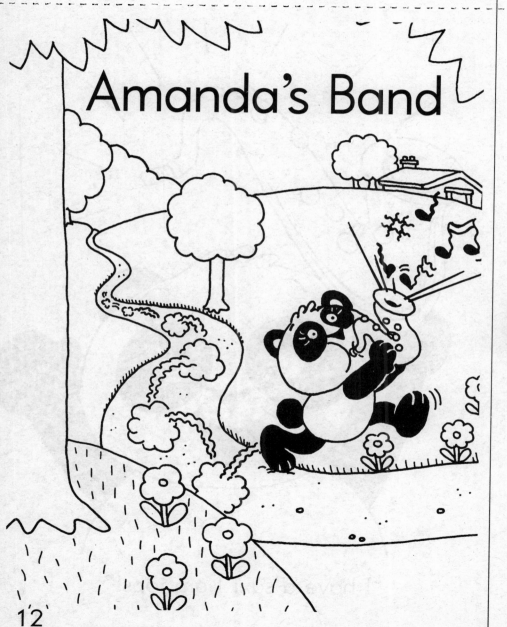

"I am damp and hot!
I have to stop!"

"I have a sax! I am tops!"

"A sax?"
"Yes, a sax!"

Amanda spots Tom Cat and his sax.

"You are tops, Tom Cat," says Amanda.
"You have a sax,
and a band,
and tons of fans."

Tom Cat hands Amanda a sax.
"Drop the mop," he says.
"Here, have a sax!"

Dad mops, and Mom pats the spot.

Have child read this book to you, sign here, and return ______________________

The Spot

by Lucy Shepard
illustrated by Olivia Cole

Columbus, OH

The McGraw-Hill Companies

MHEonline.com

SRA
Imprint 2012

Printed in the United States of America.

Send all inquiries to:
SRA/McGraw-Hill
8787 Orion Place
Columbus, OH 43240-4027

The McGraw-Hill Companies

Dad mops the spot.

Dad has his mop.

Mom has a pot.

Mom's pot is hot.

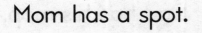

Mom has a spot.

Bob pants.

Have child read this book to you, sign here, and return ____________________

SRA Early Interventions in Reading

Bob at Bat

by Nicole Michael
illustrated by Len Epstein

Columbus, OH

The McGraw-Hill Companies

SRA Early Interventions in Reading

MHEonline.com

SRA

Imprint 2012

Printed in the United States of America.

Send all inquiries to:
SRA/McGraw-Hill
8787 Orion Place
Columbus, OH 43240-4027

The McGraw-Hill Companies

Bob bats.

Bob stands and nods.

Bob is at bat.

Bob stamps.

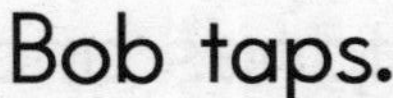

Bob taps.

Pam's map!

Have child read this book to you, sign here, and return ______________________

SRA Early Interventions in Reading

The Map

by Lucy Shepard
illustrated by Olivia Cole

Columbus, OH

The McGraw·Hill Companies

SRA Early Interventions in Reading

MHEonline.com

McGraw Hill SRA

Imprint 2012

Printed in the United States of America.

Send all inquiries to:
SRA/McGraw-Hill
8787 Orion Place
Columbus, OH 43240-4027

The McGraw-Hill Companies

Sam pats Pam's map.

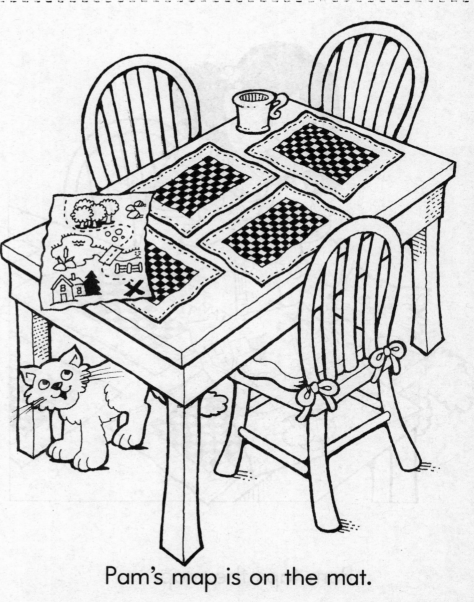

Sam taps Pam's map.

Pam's map is on the mat.

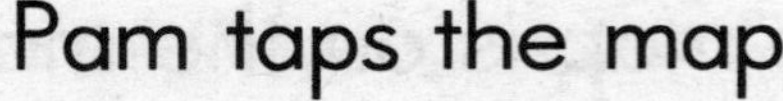

Pam taps the map.

Sam stamps on Pam's map.

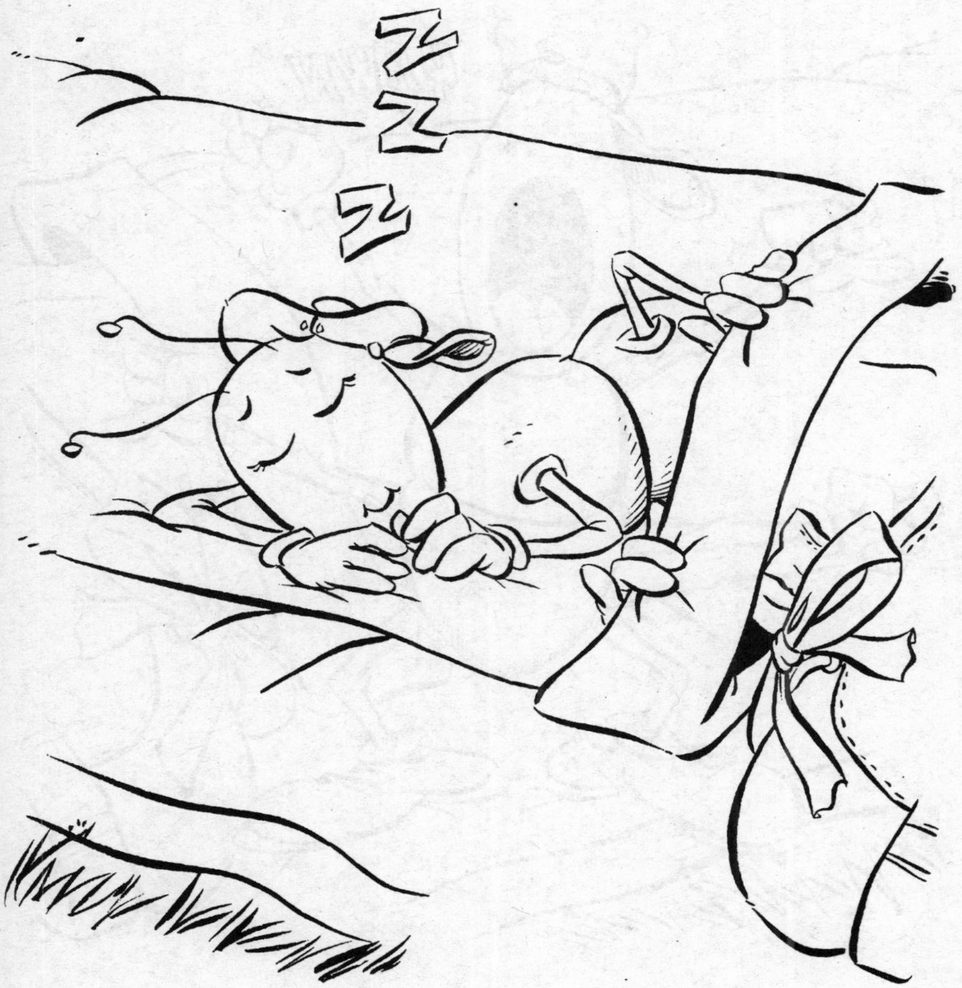

Snap naps.

SRA Early Interventions in Reading

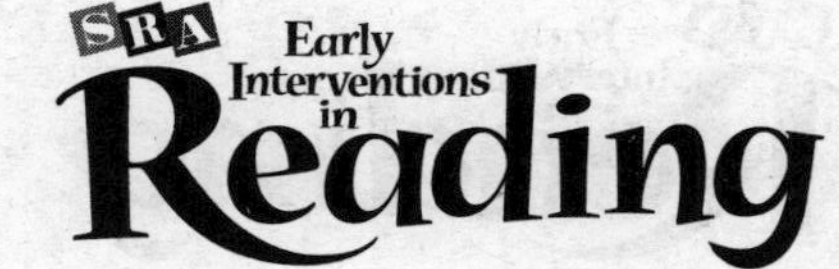

Have child read this book to you, sign here, and return ____________________

SRA Early Interventions in Reading

Snap the Ant

by Nicole Michael
illustrated by Len Epstein

SRA
Columbus, OH
The McGraw-Hill Companies

MHEonline.com

Mc Graw Hill SRA

Imprint 2012

Printed in the United States of America.

Send all inquiries to:
SRA/McGraw-Hill
8787 Orion Place
Columbus, OH 43240-4027

The McGraw-Hill Companies

Snap is by Pam's pants.

Snap sips.

Snap is an ant.

Snap is on Pam's pan.

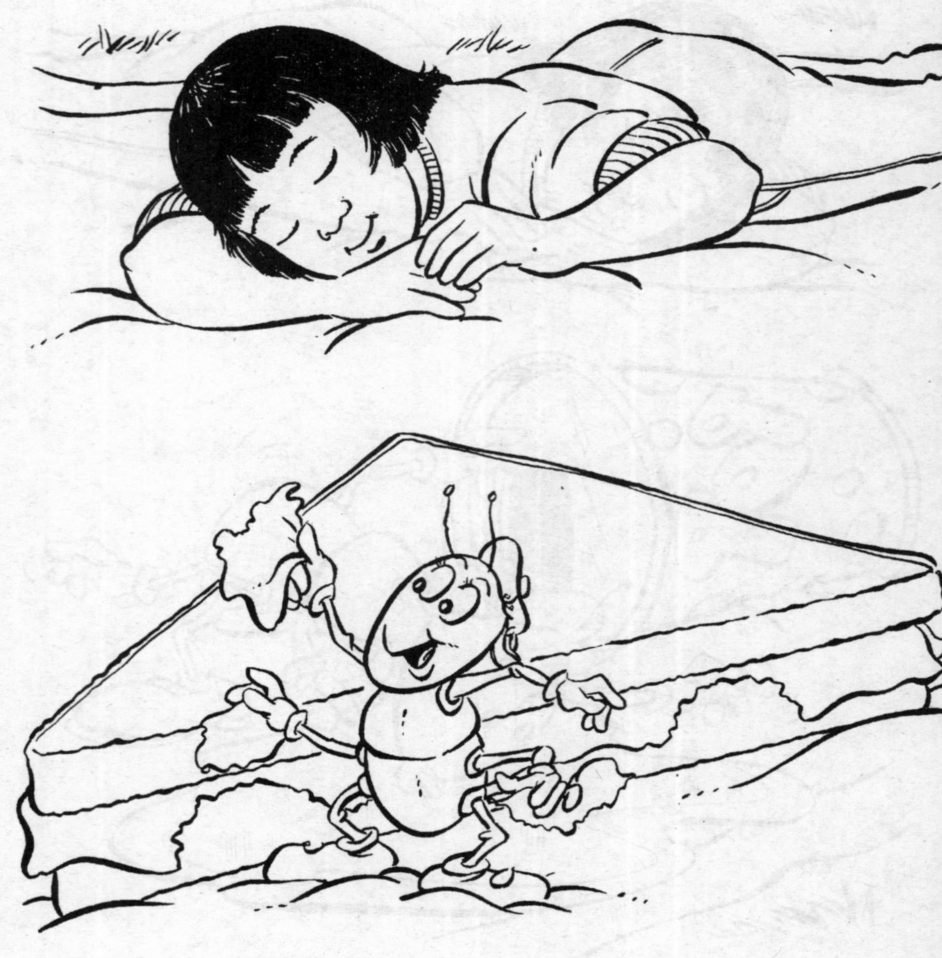

Snap has Pam's ham.

The cab stops, and in hops Dan.

Have child read this book to you, sign here, and return ______________________

The Cab

by Nancy James
illustrated by Len Epstein

Columbus, OH

The McGraw-Hill Companies

MHEonline.com

SRA

Imprint 2012

Printed in the United States of America.

Send all inquiries to:
SRA/McGraw-Hill
8787 Orion Place
Columbus, OH 43240-4027

The McGraw-Hill Companies

Dan nods.

The cab scats, and Dan taps.

Dan stands.

The cab spins past Dan.

Dan snaps.

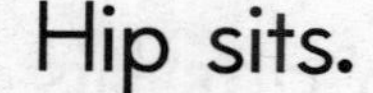

Hip sits.

Have child read this book to you, sign here, and return ______________________

Hip

by Nancy Thomas
illustrated by Len Epstein

Columbus, OH

The McGraw-Hill Companies

MHEonline.com

McGraw Hill SRA

Imprint 2012

Printed in the United States of America.

Send all inquiries to:
SRA/McGraw-Hill
8787 Orion Place
Columbus, OH 43240-4027

The McGraw-Hill Companies

Hip hits his hat.

Hip stamps.

Hip has a hat.

Hip tips his hat.

Hip taps.

Dad, Nick, and Pam picnic!

Have child read this book to you, sign here, and return ______________________

SRA Early Interventions in Reading

Picnic

by Pam Matthews
illustrated by Olivia Cole

SRA
Columbus, OH
The McGraw·Hill Companies

SRA Early Interventions in Reading

MHEonline.com

McGraw Hill SRA

Imprint 2012

Printed in the United States of America.

Send all inquiries to:
SRA/McGraw-Hill
8787 Orion Place
Columbus, OH 43240-4027

The McGraw-Hill Companies

Pam has the picnic sack.

Nick stands in sand.

Dad can pick snacks.

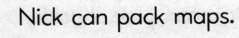

Nick can pack maps.

Pam is in the back.

I am not big!

Have child read this book to you, sign here, and return ____________

The Bug

by Janet Klausner
illustrated by Ellen Joy Sasaki

MHEonline.com

Imprint 2012

Printed in the United States of America.

Send all inquiries to:
SRA/McGraw-Hill
8787 Orion Place
Columbus, OH 43240-4027

The McGraw·Hill Companies

What is in the bag?

A bug.

But the bug! Is the bug big?

Big bugs bump in bags.

No! Is a big bug in the bag?

A big bag has the bug.

Is it big?

The bag is big.

No! The bug!
Is the bug big?

In the bag?

Yes. Is the bug
in the bag big?

It is a big
bug bag.

Have child read this book to you, sign here, and return ____________________

My Trip

by Alice Cary

illustrated by Kate Flanagan

Columbus, OH

The McGraw-Hill Companies

MHEonline.com

McGraw Hill SRA

Imprint 2012

Printed in the United States of America.

Send all inquiries to:
SRA/McGraw-Hill
8787 Orion Place
Columbus, OH 43240-4027

The McGraw-Hill Companies

I camped and tramped.
But the fox had a picnic.

For my trip, I packed a backpack.
I had a map.
I tramped and stamped.

I tracked a fox.
My picnic!

My backpack!
No picnic! No snack!

I sat on a rock.
I had a snack.

I picked a spot.
I fixed my bag.

I camped.
It was damp and hard.

Have child read this book to you, sign here, and return ____________

Zip on the Run

by Alice Cary
illustrated by Benton Mahan

Columbus, OH

The McGraw-Hill Companies

MHEonline.com

McGraw Hill SRA

Imprint 2012

Printed in the United States of America.

Send all inquiries to:
SRA/McGraw-Hill
8787 Orion Place
Columbus, OH 43240-4027

The McGraw-Hill Companies

Zip sits in a tub of suds.

The bus runs on,
but Zip does not run.

The sun is up.
Zip is on the run.

Zip mops and dusts his hut.
He hums as he runs. It is fun!

Stuck in the muck!
This run was no fun.

Zip runs for the bus.
The bus zigs and zags.
Zip sits in the muck.

A cup and a bun,
and Zip is back on the run.

A truck hits the mud.
The mud hits Zip.

Zip does not stop.
He runs and runs.

"Do not fuss," said Zack.
"Grab a pot! Grab a stick!
Start a band!" he said.
And Zack the One-Man Band
got back on his bus.

Have child read this book to you, sign here, and return ______________________

Zack the One-Man Band

by Diane Zaga
illustrated by Rusty Fletcher

MHEonline.com

SRA

Imprint 2012

Printed in the United States of America.

Send all inquiries to:
SRA/McGraw-Hill
8787 Orion Place
Columbus, OH 43240-4027

SRA
Columbus, OH

The McGraw-Hill Companies

Gus and Cass sat on a rock.
ZAP! POP! SNAP!
"What is it?" said Cass.
"What is the fuss?"

Zack huffed and puffed.
"I must stop," he said.

BAM! BUZZ! BOP!
The band started up.
"Zack, you are grand!" said Cass.
"What a band!"

"It is a bus," said Gus.
"It is a bus, and a man,
and a big brass band!"

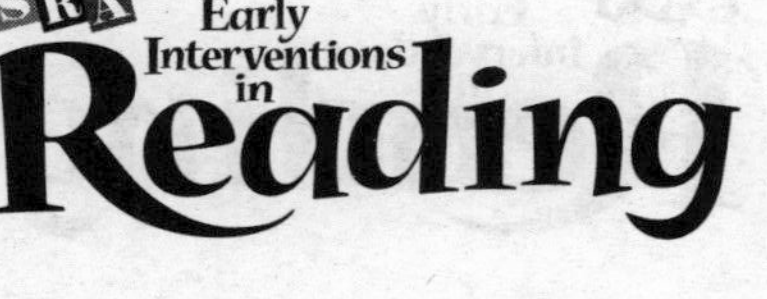

The man on the bus said,
"I am Zack the One-Man Band,
and here is my big brass band!"

"Sit here on the grass.
You can hum. You can tap.
You can drum and snap."

One hippo is in the pond.

Have child read this book to you, sign here, and return ____________________

In the Pond

by Linda Cave
illustrated by Margot Apple

Columbus, OH

The McGraw-Hill Companies

SRA Early Interventions in Reading

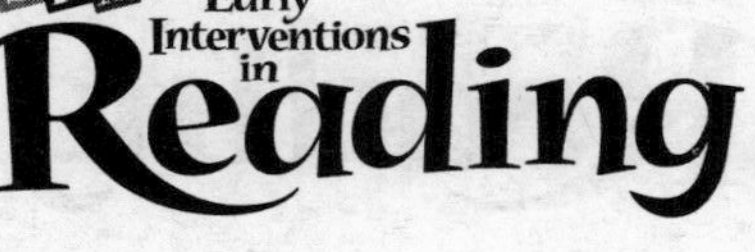

MHEonline.com

McGraw-Hill SRA

Imprint 2012

Printed in the United States of America.

Send all inquiries to:
SRA/McGraw-Hill
8787 Orion Place
Columbus, OH 43240-4027

The McGraw-Hill Companies

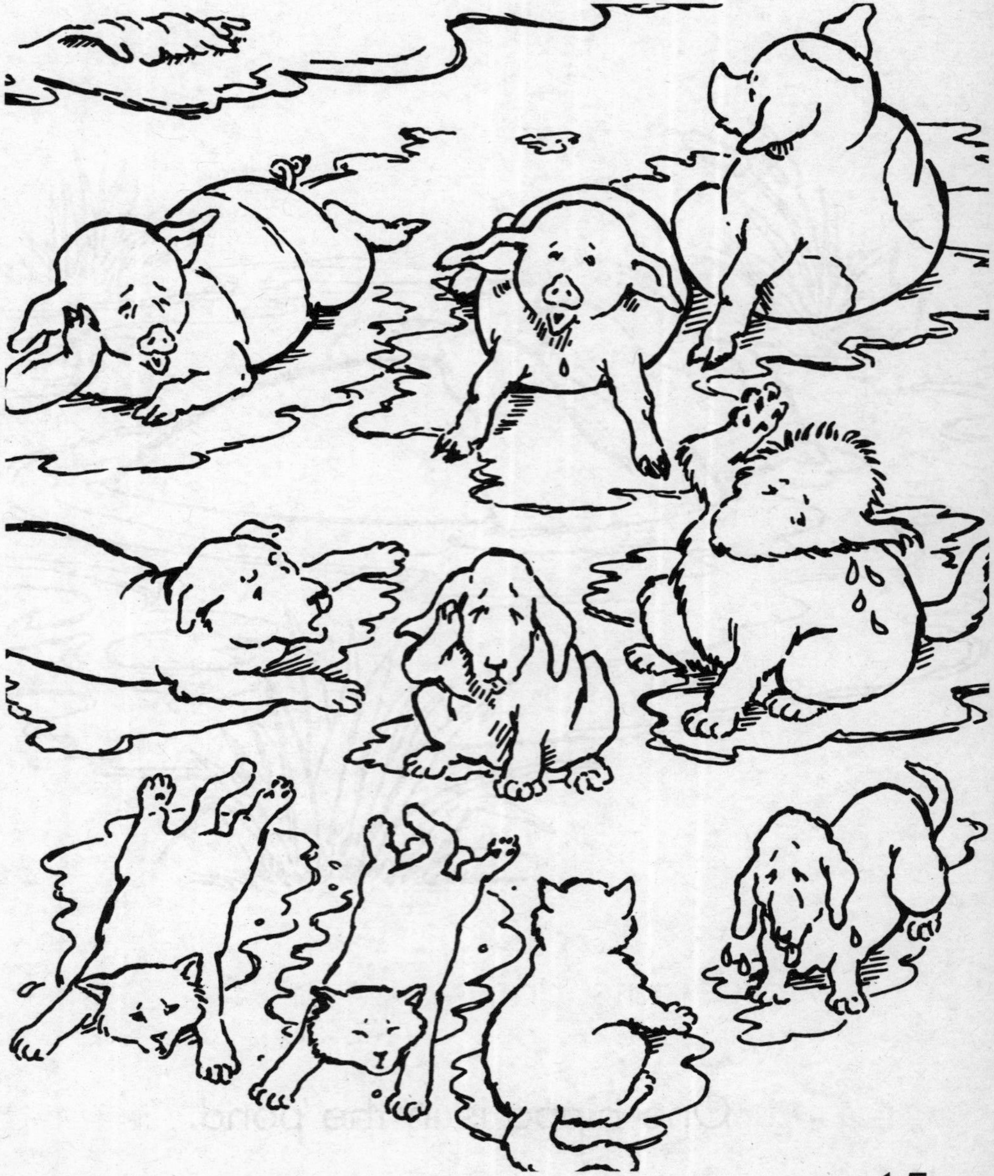

"It is hot," said the five pigs,
four dogs,
three cats, and
two bats.
"It is too hot!"

"It is hot," said five pigs.
"It is too hot!"

The pigs hopped into the pond.
Five pigs are in the pond.

“Not in the pond!” said the three cats.
“Not in the pond!” said the two bats.

"Not in the pond!" said the five pigs.
"Not in the pond!" said the four dogs.

"It is hot," said four dogs.
"It is too hot!"

The dogs hopped into the pond.
Five pigs and four dogs are in the pond.

"It is hot," said one hippo.
"It is too hot!"

The bats hopped into the pond.
Five pigs,
four dogs,
three cats, and
two bats are
in the pond.

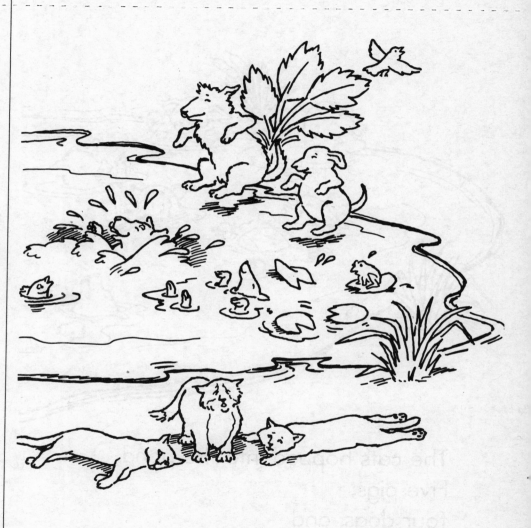

"It is hot," said three cats.
"It is too hot!"

The cats hopped into the pond.
Five pigs,
four dogs, and
three cats are
in the pond.

"It is hot," said two bats.
"It is too hot!"

"No," Meg said back.
"You would all get too damp!"
And Meg and the sled sped on.

Have child read this book to you, sign here, and return ______________________

Meg's Sled

by Dottie Raymer
illustrated by Rose Mary Berlin

MHEonline.com

SRA

Imprint 2012

Printed in the United States of America.

Send all inquiries to:
SRA/McGraw-Hill
8787 Orion Place
Columbus, OH 43240-4027

SRA
Columbus, OH

The McGraw-Hill Companies

Meg pulled a sled up the hill.
She passed an ox.
"Ox," said Meg, "help me pull this sled."
"I can't," said the ox.
"My back would get damp."

Meg sped past the bobcat.
"Meg!" said the bobcat. "Let me hop on!"
Meg sped past the ox.
"Meg!" said the ox. "Let me hop on!"

Meg sped past the bulldog.
"Meg!" said the bulldog. "Let me hop on!"

Meg pulled and pulled.
She passed a bobcat.
"Bobcat," said Meg,
"help me pull this sled."
"I can't," said the bobcat.
"My legs would get damp."

Meg pulled and pulled.
She passed a bulldog.
"Bulldog," said Meg,
"help me pull this sled."
"I can't," said the bulldog.
"My neck would get damp."

Meg got to the top.
She unpacked the sled.
She stepped onto the sled.
Away she sped.

Tess must step out.
She has to rest.
"No problem!" says Tess.
"No problem at all!"

Have child read this book to you, sign here, and return ______________

The Stand

by Alice Cary
illustrated by Rusty Fletcher

MHEonline.com

SRA

Imprint 2012

Printed in the United States of America.

Send all inquiries to:
SRA/McGraw-Hill
8787 Orion Place
Columbus, OH 43240-4027

SRA
Columbus, OH

The McGraw-Hill Companies

Step up! Step up!
Tess has a stand!
Tess can help!

Deb can't paddle in the pond.
"No problem!" says Tess.
"Rent a raft."

Kana has no pocket.
"No problem!" says Tess.
"This belt should fit you."

Tess helps all the animals.
No problem is too big.
No problem is too small.

T. Rex wants a snack.
"No problem!" says Tess.
"A big salad should fill you up."

Greg's neck is stiff.
"No problem!" says Tess.
"A scarf should do the trick."

"Here!" said Wendell.
"Next to me!"

Have child read this book to you, sign here, and return ____________

Wendell's Pets

by Anne and Robert O'Brien
illustrated by Ellen Joy Sasaki

SRA
Columbus, OH
The McGraw-Hill Companies

MHEonline.com

Mc Graw Hill SRA

Imprint 2012

Printed in the United States of America.

Send all inquiries to:
SRA/McGraw-Hill
8787 Orion Place
Columbus, OH 43240-4027

The McGraw-Hill Companies

"Where will you put all the pets, Wendell?" said Mr. Allen.

When the pets went to class,
the class was glad.
But Mr. Allen was not.

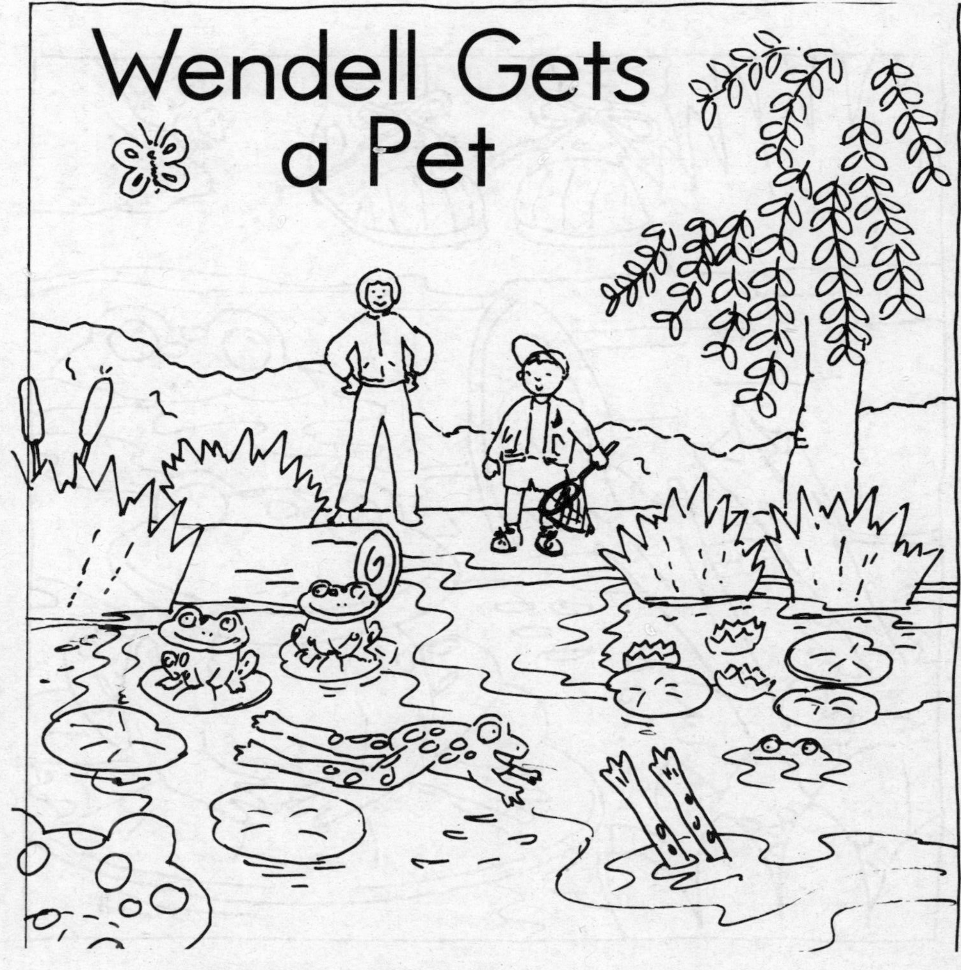

Wendell Gets a Pet

Wendell wanted a pet.
He got his net and went to the pond.

Frogs swam in the pond.
One frog was on a pad.

He had a rabbit and a lizard.
He had frogs and a tub of bugs.

Wendell had lots of pets.
He had a cat and a duck.

Wendell grabbed his net.
He stepped on a log
to get next to the frog.

He dipped his net into the pond.
The frogs swam away.

Wendell's Pets

The log was wet,
and Wendell slipped.

Wendell fell off the log.
He landed in the pond.
His net fell to the bottom.

Wendell was wet,
but he got lots of pets!

"It turned into carrot bread," said Uncle Art.
"Carrot bread! Hurray!" yelled Bert.
"Have a glass of milk, Bert," said Uncle Art.

Have child read this book to you, sign here, and return ______________________

SRA Early Interventions in Reading

What Is It?

by Patricia Griffith
illustrated by Tony Caldwell

MHEonline.com

Mc Graw Hill SRA

Imprint 2012

Printed in the United States of America.

Send all inquiries to:
SRA/McGraw-Hill
8787 Orion Place
Columbus, OH 43240-4027

The McGraw-Hill Companies

Uncle Art picked up the mixer.
“Hand me the butter, Bert,” said Uncle Art,
“and we will stir in the milk.”

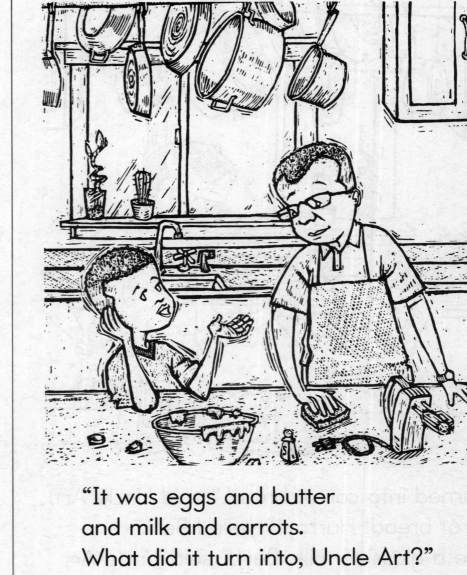

“It was eggs and butter
and milk and carrots.
What did it turn into, Uncle Art?”

"What is it?" wondered Bert.
"What is this wonderful smell?"

Uncle Art put the butter and milk into the mixer.
WHIR!
"What is it?" wondered Bert.
"Hand me the eggs, Bert," Uncle Art said, "and we will stir in a little salt."

Uncle Art put the eggs and salt into the mixer.
WHIR!
"What is it?" wondered Bert.
"Hand me the carrots, Bert," said Uncle Art.
"We will stir in the nuts too."

Uncle Art put the carrots and nuts into the mixer.
WHIR!
"What is it?" wondered Bert.
"Hand me the pan, Bert," said Uncle Art.
"We can put the batter in it."

The cars are not stuck.
There is not a jam.

Have child read this book to you, sign here, and return ____________________

In a Jam

by Dennis Fertig
illustrated by Mark Corcoran

MHEonline.com

Imprint 2012

Printed in the United States of America.

Send all inquiries to:
SRA/McGraw-Hill
8787 Orion Place
Columbus, OH 43240-4027

Columbus, OH

The McGraw-Hill Companies

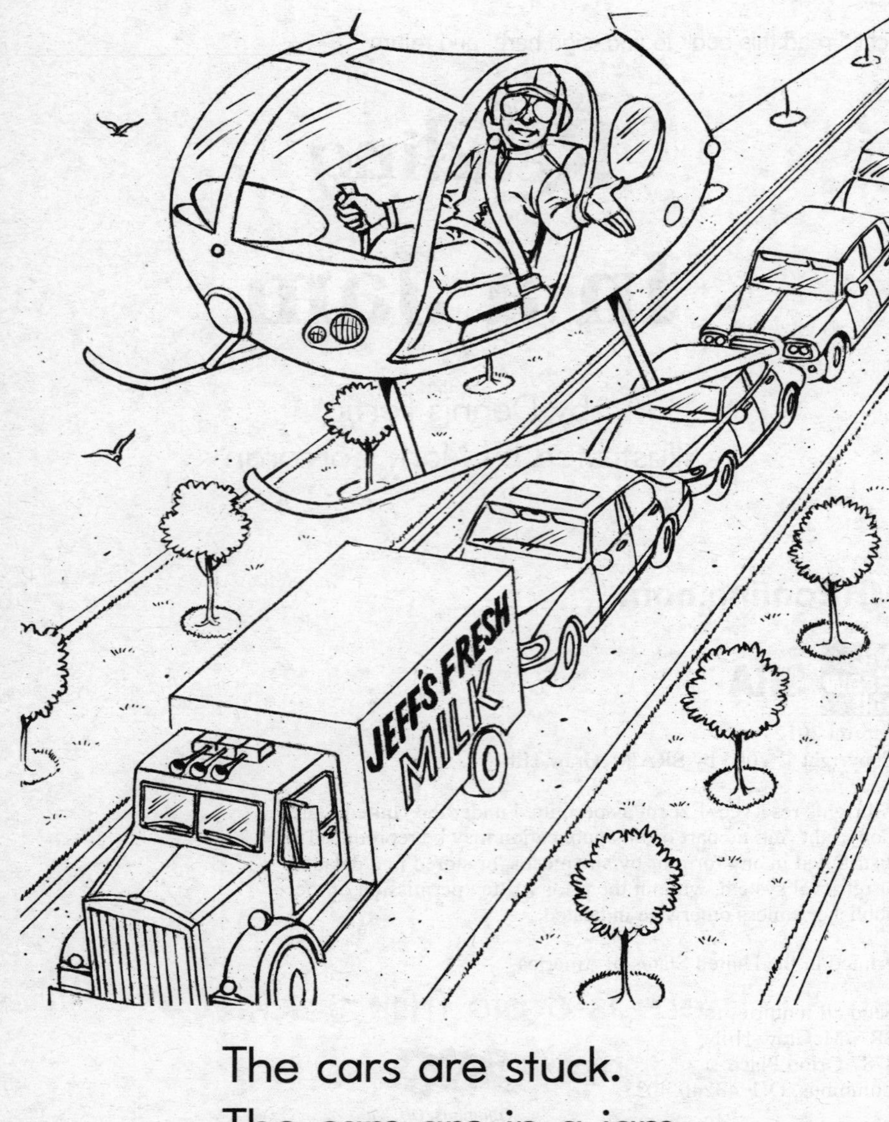

The cars are stuck.
The cars are in a jam.

Jan can.
The milk truck can run.

Can Jan start the milk truck?
Can Jan get the truck to run?

There is a big milk truck.
It will not run.
What a mess.

The cars are stuck in a jam.
A jam is not fun.

The cars are still stuck.
But here is Jan.

Ted pulled his hen out of the bucket.
He petted her head and fed her.
"I should mend this pen!" Ted said.
And he did.

Have child read this book to you, sign here, and return ______________________

Hen in a Pen

by Amy Goldman Koss
illustrated by Rose Mary Berlin

MHEonline.com

Imprint 2012

Printed in the United States of America.

Send all inquiries to:
SRA/McGraw-Hill
8787 Orion Place
Columbus, OH 43240-4027

Columbus, OH

The McGraw·Hill Companies

Ted had a hen in a pen.
The hen was Henetta.
Henetta's pen was a mess.
It was small and dented.

Henetta flapped to the top of the pen.
But she flapped too hard
and fell into a bucket.
"Hen in a bucket!" called the animals.

“Hen on the run!” called the animals
as Henetta flapped past.
“Hen on the run!” called Ted.

Ted said he would mend
Henetta’s pen.
“I should mend it,” Ted said.

"I am fed up!" Henetta sniffed.
"Ted says he should mend my pen,
but he still does not mend it."

"I have had it!" Henetta said to
the animals.
Henetta ducked her head
and flapped out of the pen.

"All finished, Seth?" said Dad.
"Yes, Dad," said Seth.
"All finished!"

Have child read this book to you, sign here, and return ____________________

SRA Early Interventions in Reading

Seth's Bath

by Anne O'Brien
illustrated by Kate Flanagan

Columbus, OH

The McGraw-Hill Companies

MHEonline.com

McGraw Hill SRA

Imprint 2012

Printed in the United States of America.

Send all inquiries to:
SRA/McGraw-Hill
8787 Orion Place
Columbus, OH 43240-4027

The McGraw-Hill Companies

"The ship is under the water!
Abandon ship!"

“We have hit the rocks!
Get the rafts!”

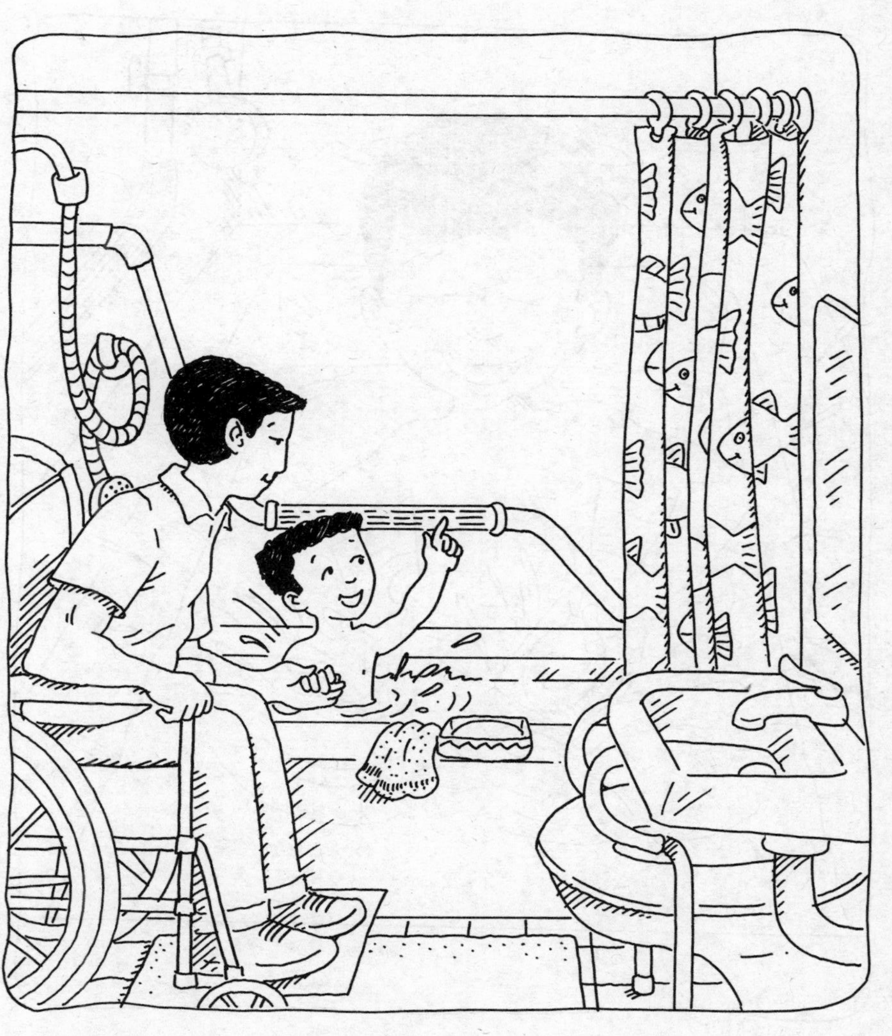

Seth stepped into the bathwater.
“To the ship!” he yelled.

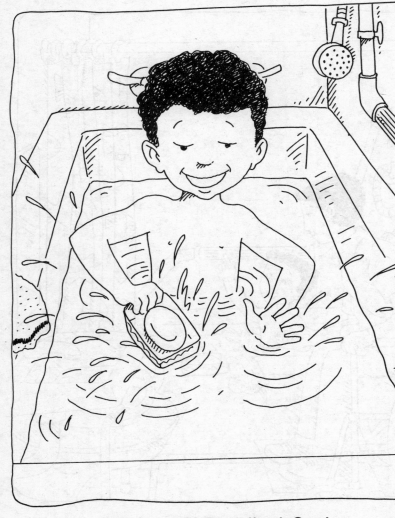

“Cast off!” called Seth.
“All hands on deck!”

“Monster fish in the water!
Man the masts!”

"Smart dog, Patch," said Elena.
"Let's do this.
Chuck can be the hitter.
I will be the pitcher.
Lil can be the catcher,
and Patch can be the fetcher!"

Have child read this book to you, sign here, and return ____________________

Patch Gets the Ball

by Anne O'Brien
illustrated by Kate Flanagan

MHEonline.com

SRA

Imprint 2012

Printed in the United States of America.

Send all inquiries to:
SRA/McGraw-Hill
8787 Orion Place
Columbus, OH 43240-4027

The McGraw-Hill Companies

Lil, Elena, and Chuck met at the ballpark.
Elena said, "I will be the pitcher.
You be the hitter, Lil.
Chuck, you can be the catcher."

Patch ran past Chuck.
He ran past the grass.
He ran past the bushes
and into the ditch.
He fetched the ball.

"Here, Patch!" Elena called to her dog.
"Fetch the ball, Patch!"

Elena pitched the ball,
and Lil hit it.
Elena ran after the ball
and tossed it to Chuck.

"Let's switch," said Chuck.
Chuck was the pitcher.
Lil was the hitter.
Elena was the catcher.
Lil hit the ball hard.
"I'll catch it!" called Chuck.

But the ball went too far,
past Chuck,
past the grass,
past the bushes,
into the ditch.

Then he called all the children and said, "Have fun!"

Have child read this book to you, sign here, and return ____________

SRA Early Interventions in Reading

The Trash Stash

by Amy Goldman Koss
illustrated by Benton Mahan

MHEonline.com

McGraw Hill SRA

Imprint 2012

Printed in the United States of America.

Send all inquiries to:
SRA/McGraw-Hill
8787 Orion Place
Columbus, OH 43240-4027

SRA
Columbus, OH

The McGraw-Hill Companies

Mitch had a stash of trash:
one dented bench,

Mitch put his stash of trash
in his garden.

five lunch boxes,
a bent drum set,
and half a sled.

a split log,
two smashed beds,

three chipped dishes,
a bit of a ship,

four strips of fishnet,
a scrap of flag,

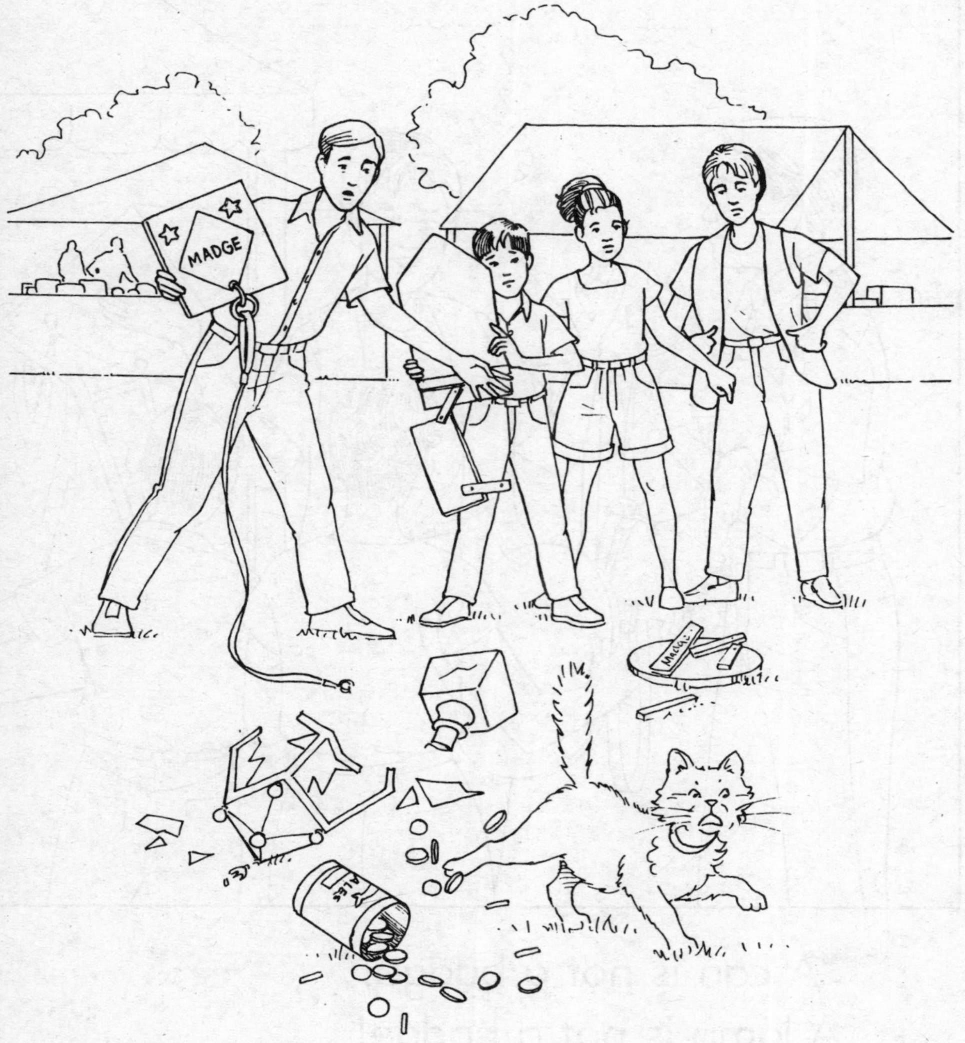

Oh no! Madge's badges!

Have child read this book to you, sign here, and return ______________________

Madge's Badges

by Marie Pickard
illustrated by Meryl Henderson

Columbus, OH

The McGraw·Hill Companies

MHEonline.com

McGraw-Hill SRA

Imprint 2012

Printed in the United States of America.

Send all inquiries to:
SRA/McGraw-Hill
8787 Orion Place
Columbus, OH 43240-4027

The McGraw-Hill Companies

“A can is not a badge!
A lamp is not a badge!
A cat is not a badge!”

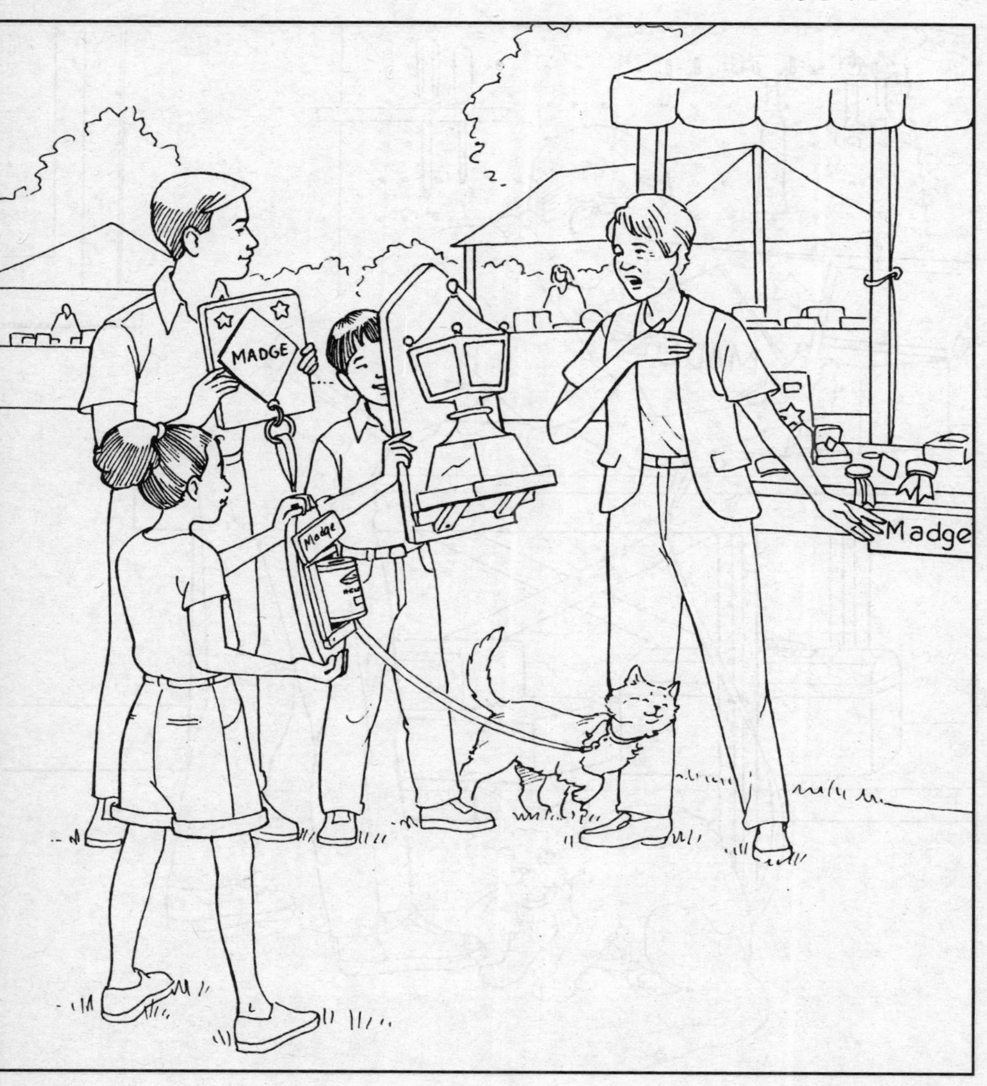

"Madge, here are badges for you!"

"I'm Madge.
I make badges at the market."

"I made a badge for Jane.
She gets nickels to help the whales."

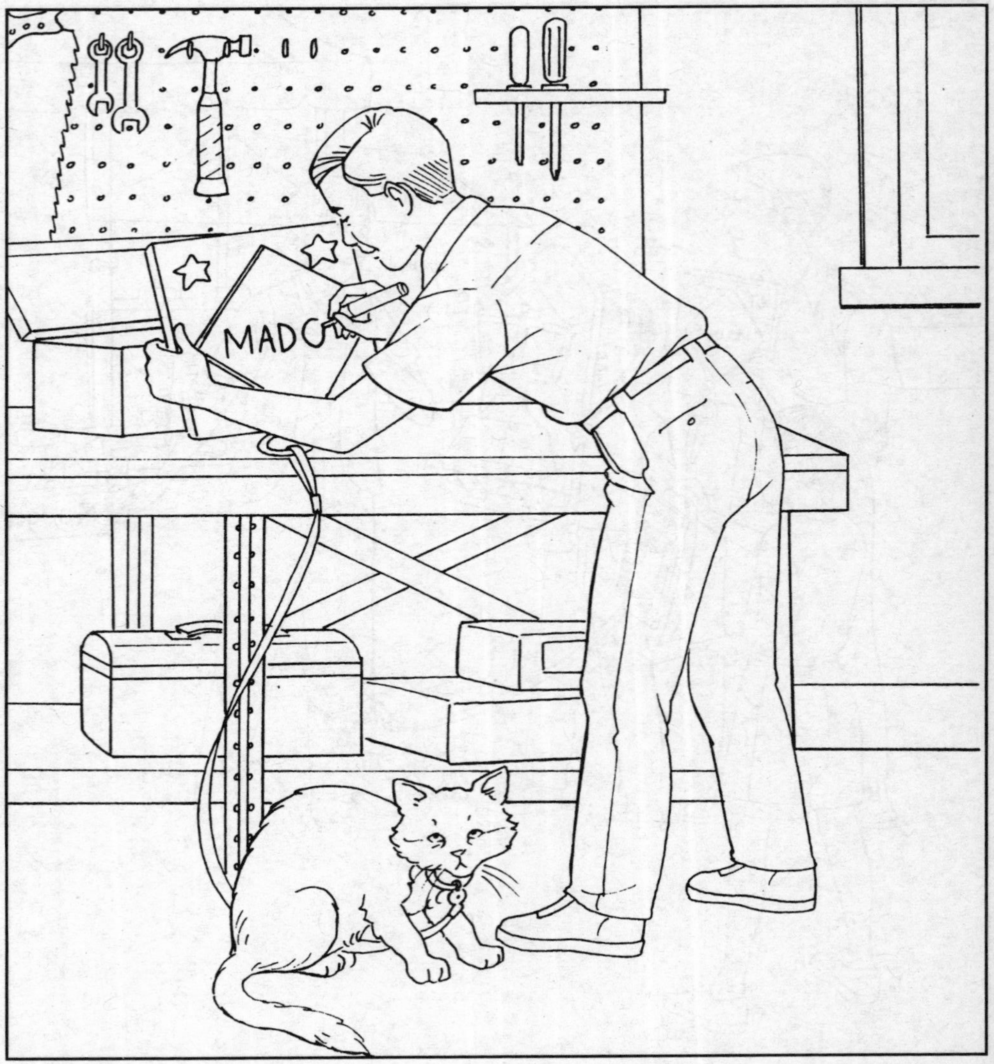

Jim made a badge with the cat.

Mitch made a badge and
scratched his lamp.

"I made a badge for Mitch.
The judge said he had the best lamp."

“Today I made a badge for Jim.
A cat was on the ledge.
Jim saved the cat.”

First Jane makes a badge with a can full of nickels.
“I will scratch Madge’s name on the badge.”

"Madge wished for a badge."
Jim asked Jane and Mitch to help.

"I make badges.
I wish I had a badge too!"

"I cannot make a badge for me."

Badges for Madge

Madge makes badges to sell.
The badge that Madge has costs a nickel.
She wishes she had a badge too.

"Hurray! They have left!" hissed Snake.
But Snake still had no fish.

Have child read this book to you, sign here, and return ____________________

Gull and Crane

by Helen Byers
illustrated by Eileen Hine

MHEonline.com

SRA

Imprint 2012

Printed in the United States of America.

Send all inquiries to:
SRA/McGraw-Hill
8787 Orion Place
Columbus, OH 43240-4027

SRA
Columbus, OH

The McGraw-Hill Companies

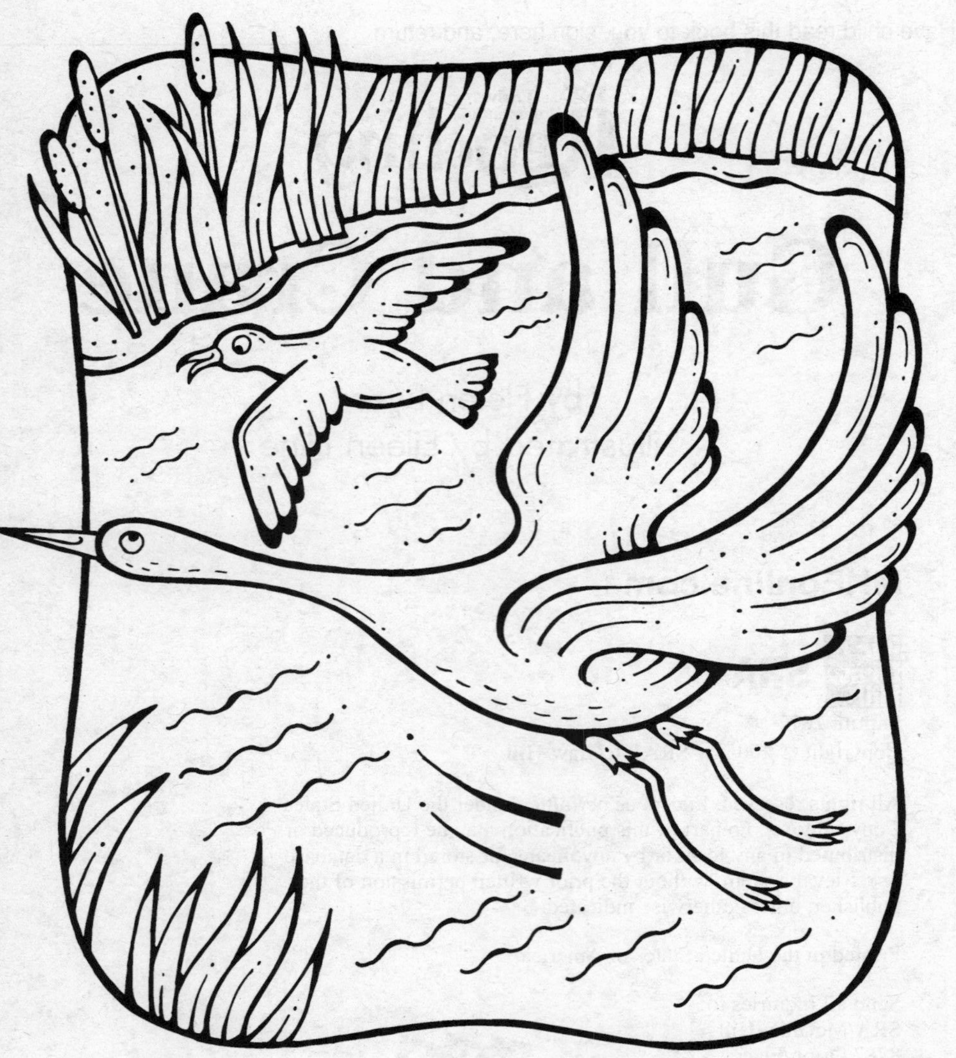

Gull and Crane were pals.

But Gull was awake. She called, "Snake in the lake! Snake in the lake! Watch the shade where you wade!"

Snake crossed the lake.
He swam into the grass
where Crane napped.

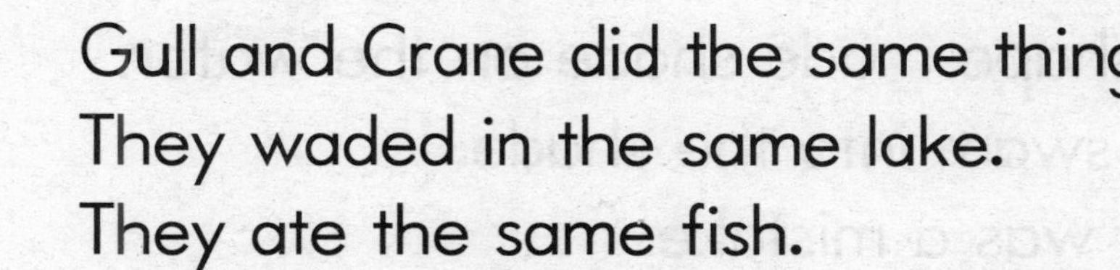

Gull and Crane did the same things.
They waded in the same lake.
They ate the same fish.

Gull and Crane fished together.
Crane waded into the lake.
His shape made shade on the water.
Fish swam into the shade.
That was a mistake.

Snake had a nest across the lake.
He was mad at Crane and Gull.
They ate Snake's fish!
"I can get rid of them," hissed Snake.

"I am glad I came too," said Jane.
"I just wish I had a jet to take me back!"

Have child read this book to you, sign here, and return ____________________

Jane and Jake

by Amy Goldman Koss
illustrated by Benton Mahan

MHEonline.com

SRA

Imprint 2012

Printed in the United States of America.

Send all inquiries to:
SRA/McGraw-Hill
8787 Orion Place
Columbus, OH 43240-4027

SRA
Columbus, OH

The McGraw-Hill Companies

Jane made fudge for Jake.
She put the fudge in a jar
to take to him.

"I am glad that you came, Jane," said Jake.
"I should not nap on the job."

Jane nudged Jake.
She jabbed him with the jar.
"Wake up, Jake! You have a job to do!"

Jane put the jar in a pack.
She trudged up to the ridge.
She trudged in the mud.

She hopped a hedge
and jumped up on a bridge.

Jake sat under the bridge.
"Jake!" called Jane. "I have fudge for you!"

Turn the page,
and I am back,
safe in my little bed.

Have child read this book to you, sign here, and return ____________________

Magic Pages

by Anne O'Brien
illustrated by Ellen Joy Sasaki

MHEonline.com

 SRA

Imprint 2012

Printed in the United States of America.

Send all inquiries to:
SRA/McGraw-Hill
8787 Orion Place
Columbus, OH 43240-4027

SRA
Columbus, OH

The McGraw-Hill Companies

When I turn my magic pages,
I can take a trip . . .

I can battle blazes
and escape!

I can watch camels run
or giraffes graze.

to a far land
to hunt for gems.

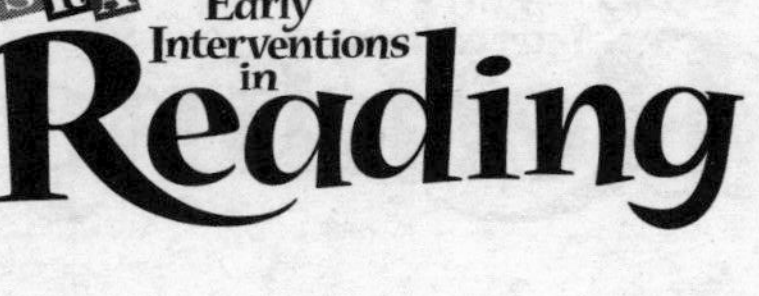

I can wade with sharks
or jump on the back
of a whale.

I can catch large snakes,
tame them,
and put them in cages.

April smiles and pats Spike.
“Spike saved my kite!” she says with pride.
“He does not like parades.
But he is a fine dog all the same.”

Have child read this book to you, sign here, and return ______________

A Fine Parade

by Anne O’Brien
illustrated by Jennifer Emery

MHEonline.com

SRA

Imprint 2012

Printed in the United States of America.

Send all inquiries to:
SRA/McGraw-Hill
8787 Orion Place
Columbus, OH 43240-4027

SRA
Columbus, OH

The McGraw-Hill Companies

Tina rides a bike.
Emma rides a trike.
Kamara skates.

Spike chases after the kite.
He finds it and takes it
back to the shed.

The parade heads up a wide path
and under a white bridge.
"My kite!" yells April.
"Where is my kite?"

Nissa pulls April and her kite
in the wagon.
It is a parade!

Where is Spike?
April finds him.
"Jump in, Spike," she says.
"It is time for the parade!"

But Spike hates parades.
He hides inside the shed.
He barks and whines.
"Do not mind him," says April.

and save
a slice for me!

Have child read this book to you, sign here, and return ____________________

Spice Cake

by Diana Zaga
illustrated by Steve Henry

MHEonline.com

Imprint 2012

Printed in the United States of America.

Send all inquiries to:
SRA/McGraw-Hill
8787 Orion Place
Columbus, OH 43240-4027

The McGraw-Hill Companies

What is this?
Spice cake?
I can make spice cake too.

Stir it a while,
and then bake it . . .

A slice or two of a
nice ripe apple.

But this does not taste like spice cake.
It has no spice!
I will help.

A shake of this.
A pinch of that.

A plate of nuts,
nine chopped dates.

"It is time to dine," said Grace.
"The spider will sit still
until an insect hits the web.
It wants a nice snack."

"Me too!" said Mike. "It is time for lunch!"

Have child read this book to you, sign here, and return ____________________

The Spider Club

by Alice Cary
illustrated by Diane Blasius

Columbus, OH

The McGraw-Hill Companies

MHEonline.com

McGraw Hill SRA

Imprint 2012

Printed in the United States of America.

Send all inquiries to:
SRA/McGraw-Hill
8787 Orion Place
Columbus, OH 43240-4027

The McGraw-Hill Companies

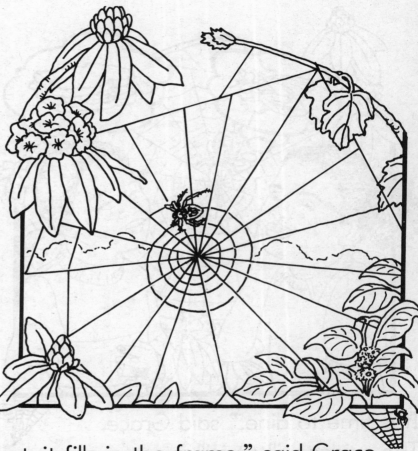

"Next, it fills in the frame," said Grace. "It spins fast."

"What a wonderful web!" said Mike. "What will it do next?"

"What next?" asked Mike.

"The spider runs from bridge to bridge," said Grace.
"It spins and spins to make a frame for the web."

"Run, Grace!" yelled Mike. "It's a spider!"
"Run?" said Grace. "What for?"
"Girls hate spiders," said Mike.

"Not me," said Grace. "I like spiders.
My sister and I have a spider club."

"This silk thread is called a dragline.
The spider rides on the end of it.
Then the spider makes two bridges."

"What a trick!" said Mike.

“A spider makes two kinds of silk.
One kind sticks to things,” said Grace.
“When an insect hits the web,
it sticks to the silk.”

“That is a garden spider,” said Grace.
“It has eight eyes!”

“It has lots of legs too,” said Mike.

“Yes, all spiders have eight legs,” said Grace.

"Are all spiders alike?" asked Mike.

Grace led Mike to the Spider Club.
Inside the club were lots of spiders.

"No, not all spiders are alike," Grace said.

"That thread is made of silk," said Grace.

"Isn't silk for shirts?" asked Mike.

"Not spider silk," said Grace.

"Here's a spider!" called Mike.

"Will it spin a web?"

"Sit still," said Grace, "and we will find out."

"Oh! It fell from the branch!" yelled Mike.

"It made a thread!"

"Here is a spider that jumps," said Grace.

"Jumps? Yikes!" said Mike.

"Not on you," said Grace. "It jumps on insects."

"Can't it spin a web?" asked Mike.

"No," said Grace, "not all spiders spin webs."

"This spider makes a trap, not a web," said Grace.
"It digs a trap and hides in it.
Insects fall into the trap."

"Which spider do you like best?" asked Mike.

"I like all kinds of spiders," said Grace.
"Crab spiders, pirate spiders, barn spiders,
spiders that fish, and spiders that spit.
But the spiders I like best
are the ones that spin webs.
Maybe we can find one outside."

The troll went home and put on the robe.
For once, he had no ice on his nose.
"I am not cold!" said the troll.
"Thank you, Mole!"

Have child read this book to you, sign here, and return ____________________

The Cold Troll

by Amy Goldman Koss
illustrated by Yuri Salzman

MHEonline.com

Imprint 2012

Printed in the United States of America.

Send all inquiries to:
SRA/McGraw-Hill
8787 Orion Place
Columbus, OH 43240-4027

SRA
Columbus, OH

The McGraw-Hill Companies

Once an old troll had a home made of stone.

Mole read the note.
"Do not mope, Troll," Mole scolded.
"Take home this robe."

HELLO, MOLE!
HELP!
I AM SO COLD!
MY STOVE HAS
FROZEN!
I HAVE ICE
ON MY NOSE!
JAKE TROLL

The old troll's home was cold.
It was so cold that ice was on his nose.
It was so cold that his stove froze.

The troll gave his broken stove a poke.
"This is no joke," he said.
"This cold is too much.
I have one last hope. I will go visit Mole."

Mole had a nice snug hole.
The cold troll wrote a note.
He slipped the note into Mole's hole.

Dad! I made a card full of roses!

A perfect surprise for Mom! Jonas, you solved the problem!

Have child read this book to you, sign here, and return ____________

The Surprise

by Alice Cary
illustrated by Rusty Fletcher

MHEonline.com

SRA

Imprint 2012

Printed in the United States of America.

Send all inquiries to:
SRA/McGraw-Hill
8787 Orion Place
Columbus, OH 43240-4027

Columbus, OH

The McGraw-Hill Companies

Dad, I have a problem.

A problem, Jonas? What is your problem?

No, she doesn't. Well, Jonas, you do have a problem.

Mom doesn't like hats.

SRA
Early Interventions in Reading

Yes, I suppose it is.
You could get her
a hat with roses on it.
It is too late, Dad.
The shop is closed.

I want to surprise Mom.
I want to get her a present.
A present,
Jonas?

I want to get her roses.
Roses? Well, you could pick roses outside.

It is too cold outside for roses, Dad.
Yes, I suppose so. You could get roses at a shop.

Cupid does not like the forest.
He does not like the bugs,
the snakes, or his huge pile.
But Cupid does like music!

Have child read this book to you, sign here, and return ____________

Cupid the Mule

by Dottie Raymer
illustrated by Elaine Garvin

MHEonline.com

Imprint 2012

Printed in the United States of America.

Send all inquiries to:
SRA/McGraw-Hill
8787 Orion Place
Columbus, OH 43240-4027

The McGraw-Hill Companies

Cupid is a mule.
He lives in a forest
close to the Amazon River.

At last Alfonso gets out his pipes.
His pipes make fine music.
The music amuses Cupid.

Cupid does not like the huge pile.
He refuses to go to the river.
Alfonso pushes and pulls,
but Cupid does not budge.

Cupid does not like the forest.
He does not like the bugs,
the snakes,
or the river animals.
But Cupid does like music.

Alfonso is a trader.
He cuts branches
and trades them at the river.
The branches are used to make
baskets and fish traps.

After Alfonso cuts the branches,
he makes a huge pile.
Then he puts the pile
on Cupid's back.

Have child read this book to you, sign here, and return ____________________

Steve's Secret

by Amy Goldman Koss
illustrated by Rusty Fletcher

MHEonline.com

SRA

Imprint 2012

Printed in the United States of America.

Send all inquiries to:
SRA/McGraw-Hill
8787 Orion Place
Columbus, OH 43240-4027

Columbus, OH

The McGraw·Hill Companies

Steve had a secret.
He hid it in his pocket.

"You will find out,"
said Steve with a smile.
"Then the secret will be yours and mine."

"What shade is it?" asked Eve.
"Is it white? Is it red?"

"What is in your pocket?" asked Eve.
"An acorn? A stone?"
"It is a secret," said Steve.
"It is for me."

"What size is it?" asked Eve.
"Is it little? Is it big?"
"It is little," said Steve.
"But it is my secret. Do not even ask."

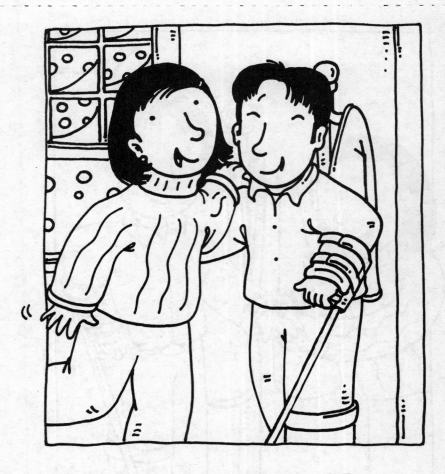

"What shape is it?" asked Eve.
"Is it flat? Is it tall?"
"It is flat," said Steve.
"But it is my secret. Let me be."

"We made a tent!" said Hugo.

"Yes, we used our heads,"
said Eva, "but let's be quick
and get inside! These bugs
make me itch!"

Have child read this book to you, sign here, and return ____________________

Eva Uses Her Head

by Robert R. O'Brien
illustrated by Linda Kelen

Columbus, OH

The McGraw-Hill Companies

SRA Early Interventions in Reading

MHEonline.com

McGraw Hill SRA

Imprint 2012

Printed in the United States of America.

Send all inquiries to:
SRA/McGraw-Hill
8787 Orion Place
Columbus, OH 43240-4027

The McGraw-Hill Companies

"I will pull on this end of the rope,"
said Eva, "and you pull on that end."

Eva and Hugo pulled on the rope.

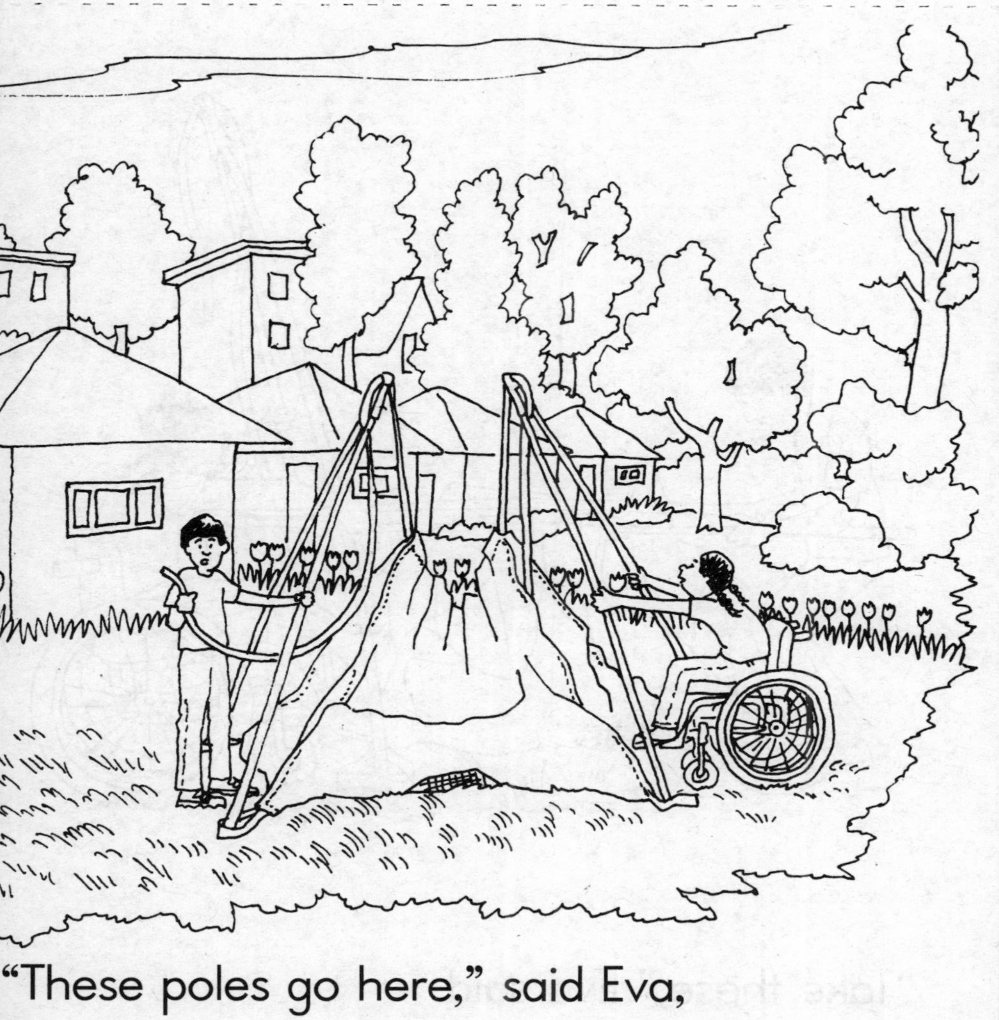

"These poles go here," said Eva,
"and those go next to you."

"Then what is the rope for?" asked Hugo.

SRA Early Interventions in Reading

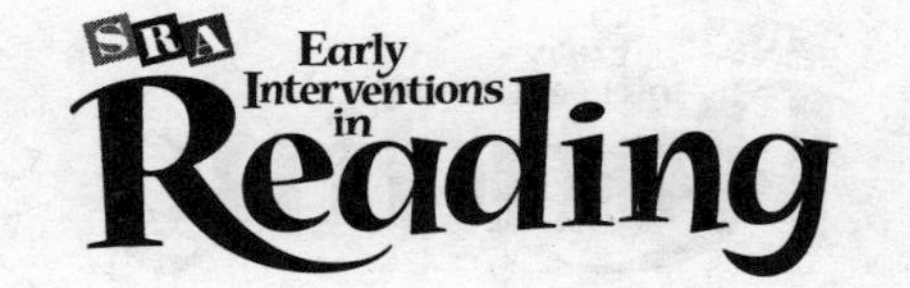

The Step Problem

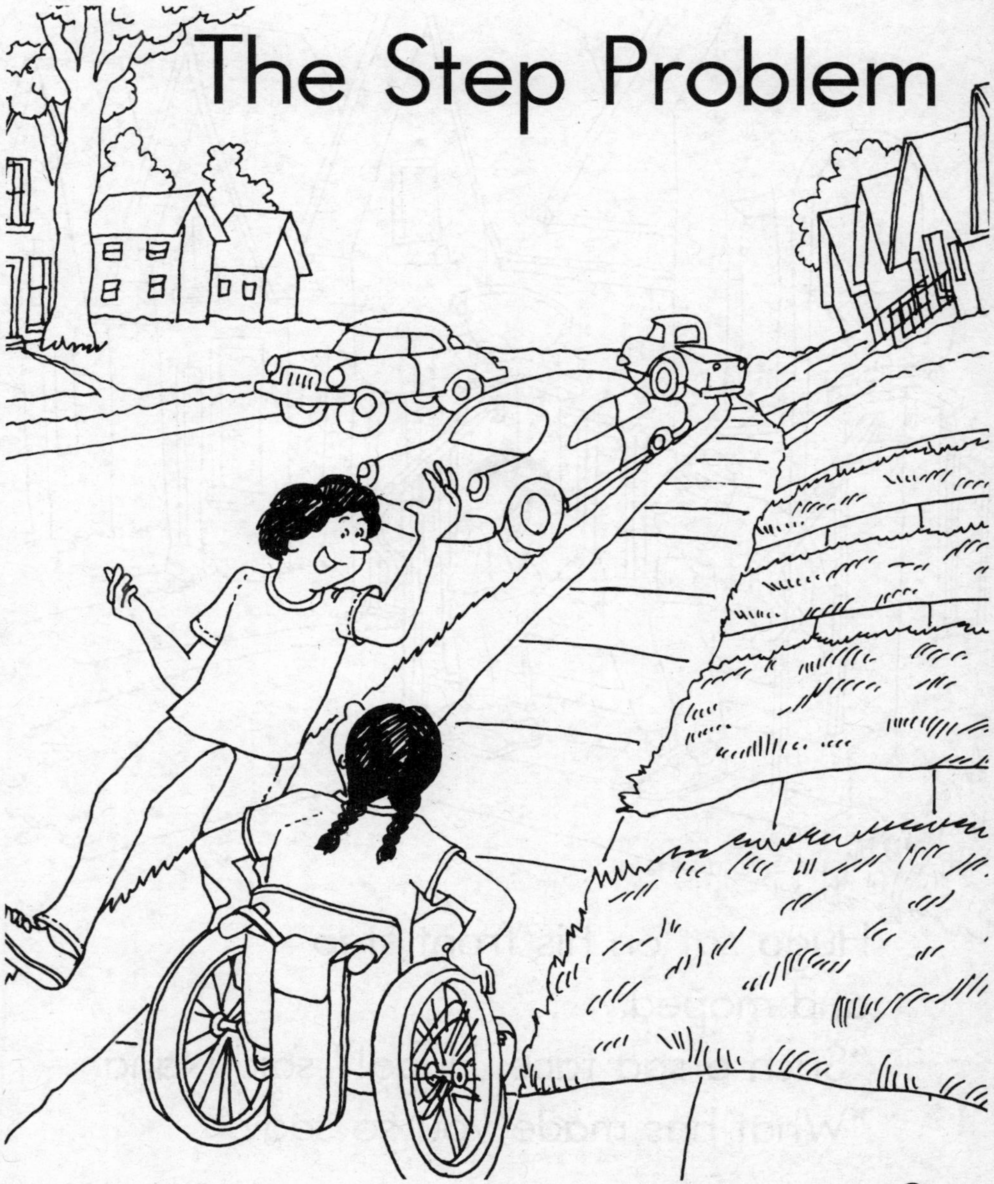

Hugo sat on his front step
and moped.
"Such a sad face, Hugo!" said Nana.
"What has made you so sad?"

"Take these," Eva said.
She held out two poles.

"What are these for?" asked Hugo.

Hugo and Eva sat in Eva's yard.
"Let's go inside," said Hugo.
"These bugs make me itch!"

"I have an idea!" said Eva.

"I want to invite Eva over,"
said Hugo, "but even if she came,
she would not be able
to get up these steps."

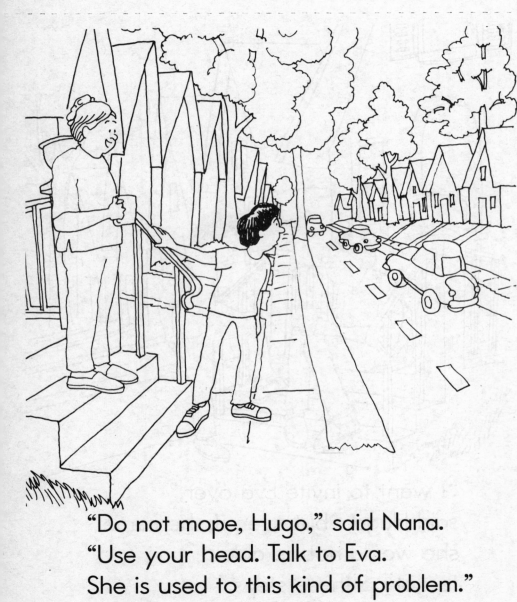

“Do not mope, Hugo,” said Nana.
“Use your head. Talk to Eva.
She is used to this kind of problem.”

The Bug Problem

Hugo talked to Eva.
"No problem!" said Eva.
"Let's go!"

"I'm glad you came," said Hugo.
"But these steps are huge.
Will we be able to get inside?"

Eva smiled.
"This is not a hard problem," she said.
"I just use my head!"

"Oh! I can breathe!" said Deana.
"I feel so much better!"
"I am glad," Dad said with a smile.
"Dragons don't get colds."

Have child read this book to you, sign here, and return ____________________

Dragons Don't Get Colds

by Dottie Raymer
illustrated by Rose Mary Berlin

MHEonline.com

SRA

Imprint 2012

Printed in the United States of America.

Send all inquiries to:
SRA/McGraw-Hill
8787 Orion Place
Columbus, OH 43240-4027

Columbus, OH

The McGraw-Hill Companies

Deana the Dragon felt terrible.
"I feel weak," said Deana.
"My nose hurts, and I can't breathe.
I can't speak. I just creak!"

"Dragons don't like tea," creaked Deana.
"Sip it," said Dad. "We will see."
The steam tickled Deana's nose.
"Dragons don't . . . AH! . . . get . . .
AH! . . . colds! . . . ACHOOOO!"
Deana sneezed a big sneeze.

"Can you breathe flames?" asked Dad.
"Well, no," creaked Deana.
Dad made a pot of tea.
"The heat will help you breathe," he said.

Deana's dad felt her cheeks.
"You feel hot," he said.
"You have a fever.
You must have a cold."

"A cold!" creaked Deana.
"Dragons don't get colds!"
"You have a cold, Deana," said Deana's dad.
"You need to go to bed."

"I don't need to go to bed," creaked Deana.
"Dragons don't get colds.
Dragons breathe flames.
Dragons don't get colds!"

The queen squid had saved her sea pals.
The shark had no meal.
The queen squid and her pals
had quite a feast!

Have child read this book to you, sign here, and return ____________________

Queen Squid and Her Sea Pals

by Sandy Loose
illustrated by Susan Nethery

MHEonline.com

SRA

Imprint 2012

Printed in the United States of America.

Send all inquiries to:
SRA/McGraw-Hill
8787 Orion Place
Columbus, OH 43240-4027

SRA
Columbus, OH

The McGraw-Hill Companies

A huge queen squid lived
in the deep, dark sea.
This kind queen squid
had a squad of sea pals to help her.

The quick queen swam to her pals.
She squirted black liquid
into the shark's face.
The shark swam away.

This time, the squad squealed!
The queen heard the squeals.

The huge queen squid squealed,
"I need a meal!"

The queen's squad of sea pals
heard her squeal.
"It's time for the queen's meal,"
said the pals.

The squad swam to get
the queen her meal.
A quiet shark swam near them.
He needed a meal too.

"Yes," said Mrs. Fay, "but to sail,
you should stay out of the water!
Here comes the rain, Ray.
Grab a pail! It is time to bail!"

Have child read this book to you, sign here, and return ____________

SRA Early Interventions in Reading

Sail Day

by Alice Cary
illustrated by Eva Cockerille

MHEonline.com

Imprint 2012

Printed in the United States of America.

Send all inquiries to:
SRA/McGraw-Hill
8787 Orion Place
Columbus, OH 43240-4027

The McGraw-Hill Companies

"Mrs. Fay! Mrs. Fay!
Today is the day!
Today I get to sail!"

"The main? The jib?
Well, I just want to sail."

“Each sail has a name,”
said Mrs. Fay. “This little one
is called the jib.”

“Hi, Ray. Yes, today is the day.
But it is quite gray today.
We should wait. It may rain.”

"Oh, I'm not afraid of rain.
We can sail in rain!"

"We can sail, but we must be safe,"
said Mrs. Fay. "Stay here, Ray.
I will check the main."

"The main?" said Ray.
"Do you mean the big sail?
I can help raise it!"

But Harry did not hear Quincy.
Harry was in a hurry.
He had to run off.
Hurry, Harry, hurry!

Have child read this book to you, sign here, and return ____________

SRA Early Interventions in Reading

Dog Dreams

by Helen Byers
illustrated by Nelle Davis

SRA
Columbus, OH
The McGraw-Hill Companies

SRA Early Interventions in Reading

MHEonline.com

McGraw-Hill SRA

Imprint 2012

Printed in the United States of America.

Send all inquiries to:
SRA/McGraw-Hill
8787 Orion Place
Columbus, OH 43240-4027

The McGraw-Hill Companies

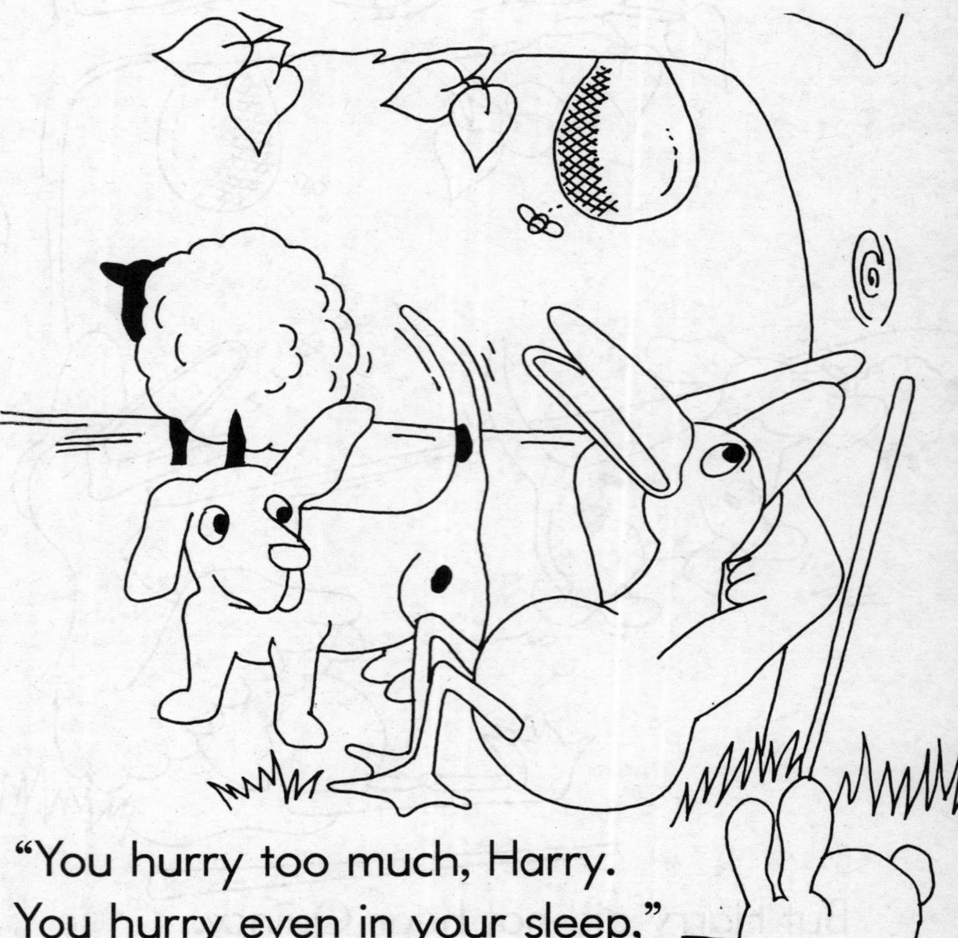

"You hurry too much, Harry.
You hurry even in your sleep,"
quacked Quincy.
"You make me feel tired.
I need a little nap."

"In the last dream, a fire trapped three sheep. I had to hurry.
Hurry, Harry, hurry!
I had to lead the sheep away from the fire!"

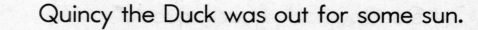

Quincy the Duck was out for some sun.

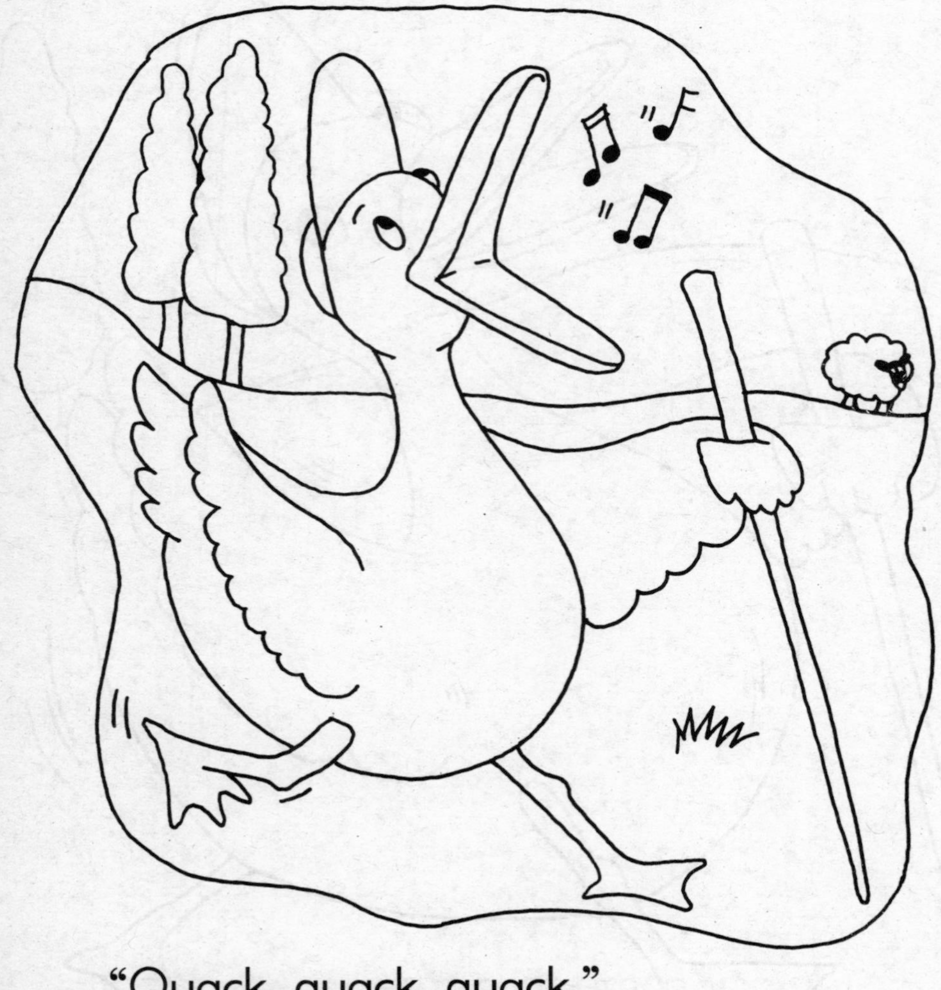

"Quack, quack, quack,"
Quincy said as he went.
"Quack, quack, quack, quack."

"In the next dream,
a queen had me chase a rabbit.
Hurry, Harry, hurry!
I had to chase away the rabbit."

"In one dream, fleas and bees
were after me. I had to hurry.
Hurry, Harry, hurry!"

Quincy came to a tree
with big green leaves.
A dog was asleep under the tree.

It was Harry!
"Quack!" said Quincy.
But Harry did not wake up.

Harry woke up. He was out of breath.
"I had a dream," said Harry.
"I had three dreams."

"Tell me your dreams," said Quincy.
"I like dream stories."

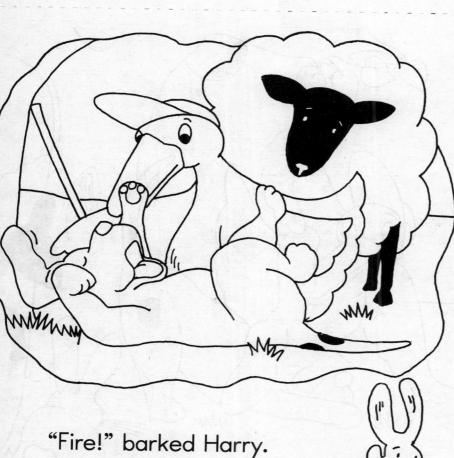

"Fire!" barked Harry.
"Hurry, Harry, hurry!"

"I have to wake him!"
said Quincy. "Wake up, Harry!
Quack, quack, quack, quack, quack!"

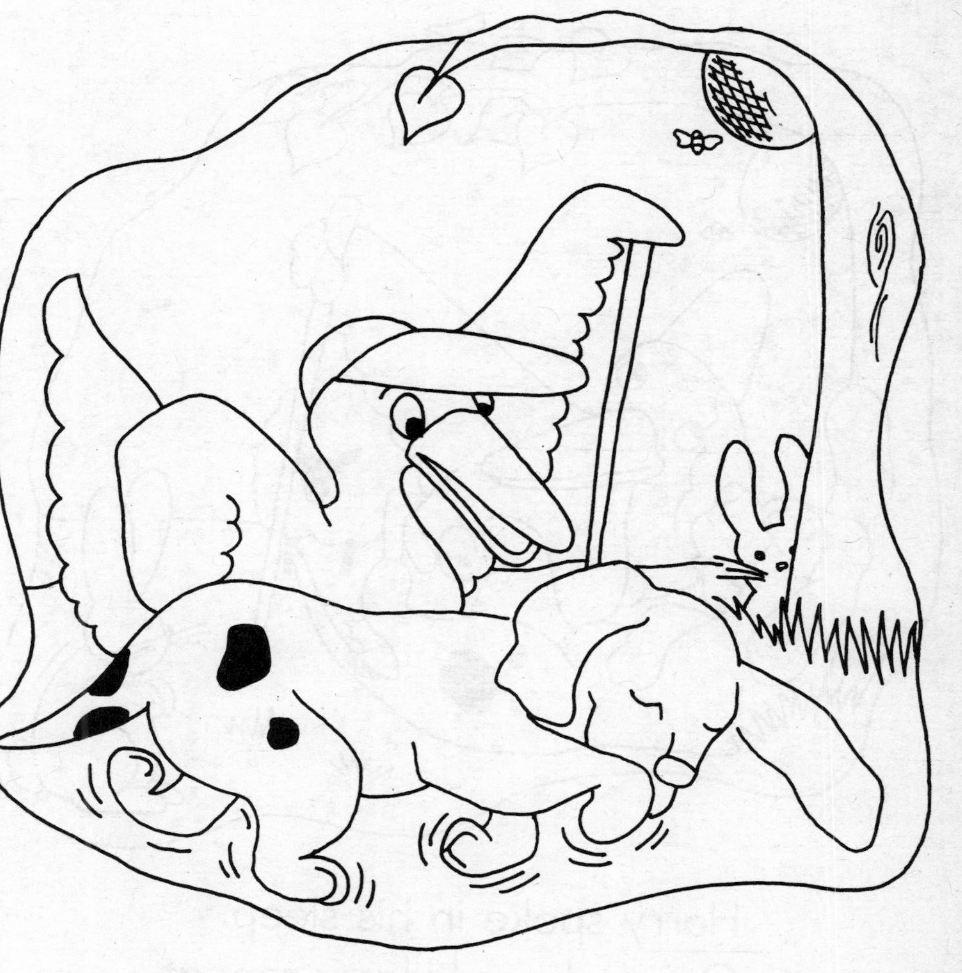

Harry was deep in a dream.
Harry's feet ran in his sleep.

Harry spoke in his sleep.
Quincy heard Harry repeat,
"Hurry, Harry, hurry!
Hurry, Harry, hurry!"

"Harry!" Quincy quacked.
"Wake up! You do not have
to hurry in your sleep!"

The fancy party is over.
The babies and teddies are muddy.
The candy is dirty. The party hats are torn.
Happy puppies lap up the ice cream.
"Thanks for the help," Willy tells his puppies.

Have child read this book to you, sign here, and return ____________

The Fancy Party

by Anne O'Brien

illustrated by Elaine Garvin

MHEonline.com

SRA

Imprint 2012

Printed in the United States of America.

Send all inquiries to:
SRA/McGraw-Hill
8787 Orion Place
Columbus, OH 43240-4027

The McGraw-Hill Companies

Nellie and Willy like to have fancy parties.
They invite Nellie's baby dolls and teddies.
Today, they have invited
Willy's puppies too.

Nellie gets out the candy and ice cream.
Willy begins to put ice cream on the plates.
"No more help, please!"
Nellie tells the puppies.

Nellie has berries from the garden.
Willy puts a big berry on every plate.
Willy's puppies help.

Nellie sets up a table in the yard.
Willy puts napkins and plates on the table.
Willy's puppies help.

Nellie gets her baby dolls and teddies.
Willy carries them to the table.
Willy's puppies help.

Nellie makes funny party hats.
Willy tapes ribbons onto each hat.
Willy's puppies help.

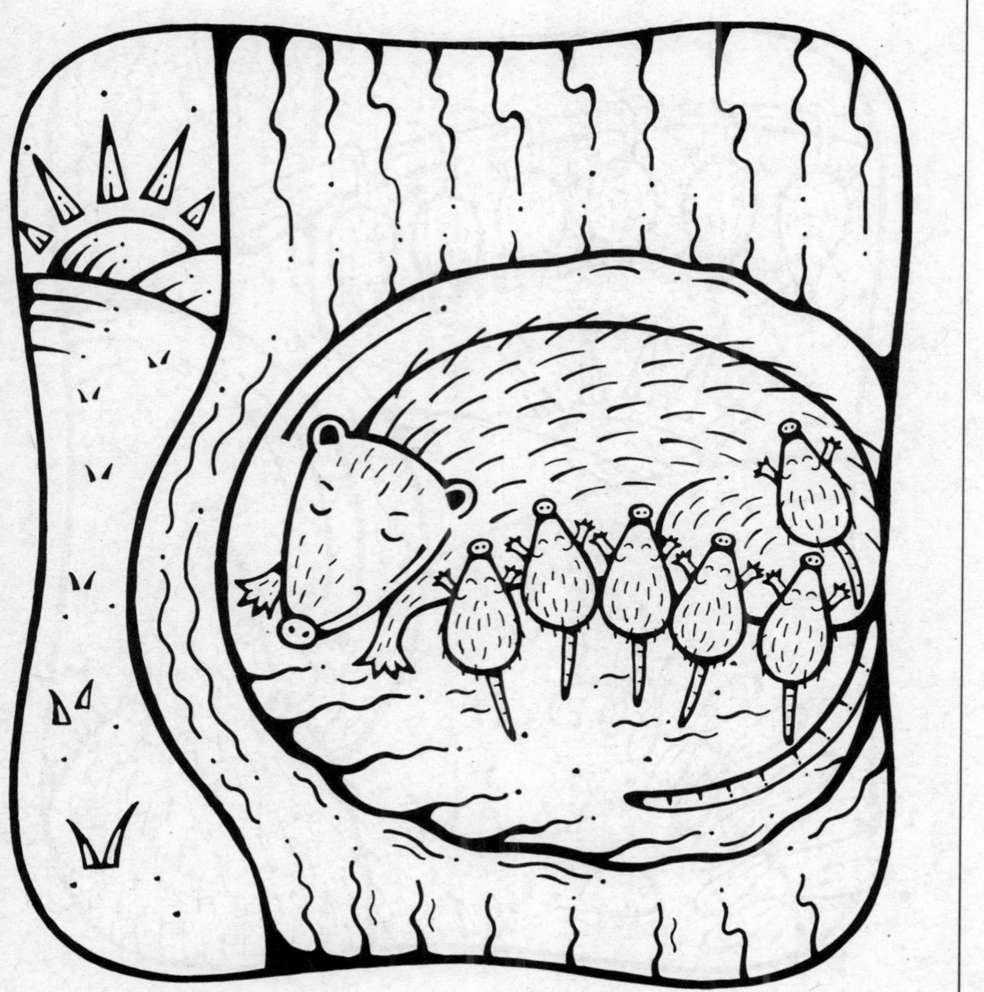

"Go to sleep," she tells her babies.
"We will play again tonight."

Have child read this book to you, sign here, and return ______________________

SRA Early Interventions in Reading

The Opossum

by Anne O'Brien
illustrated by Eileen Hine

Columbus, OH

The McGraw-Hill Companies

SRA Early Interventions in Reading

MHEonline.com

McGraw Hill SRA

Imprint 2012

Printed in the United States of America.

Send all inquiries to:
SRA/McGraw-Hill
8787 Orion Place
Columbus, OH 43240-4027

The McGraw-Hill Companies

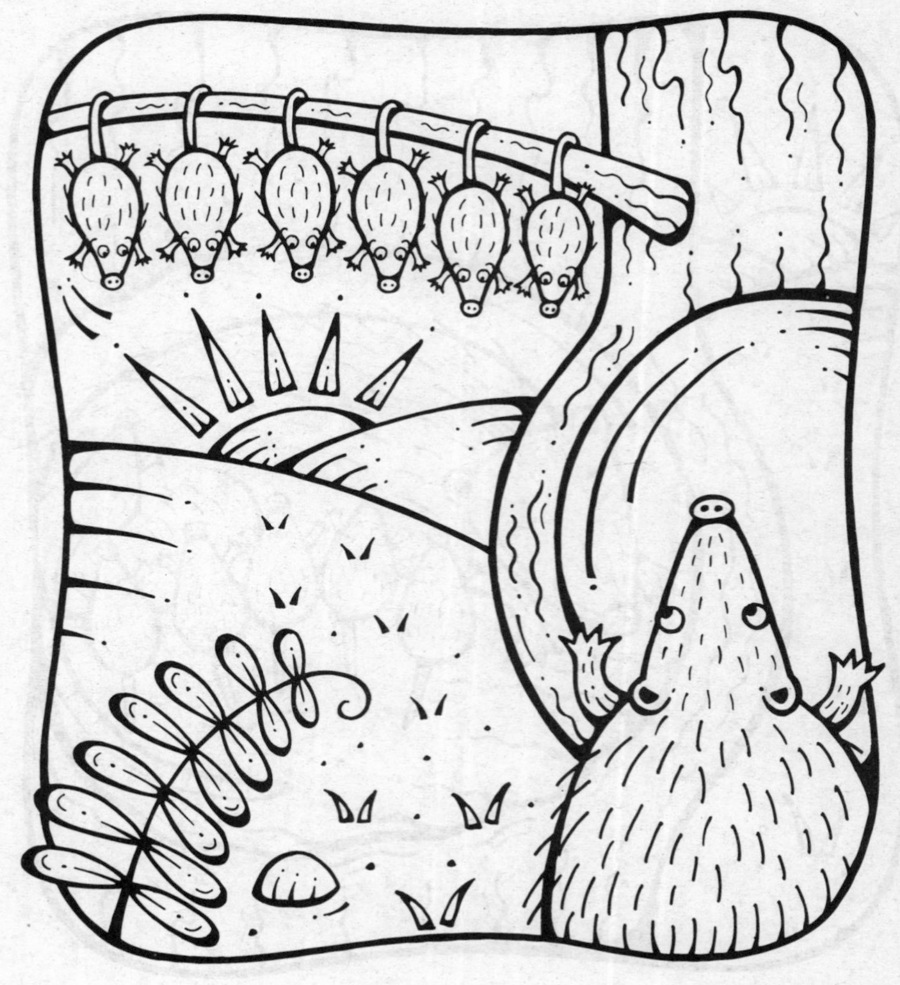

Night is over. It begins to get light.
The opossum returns to her tree.

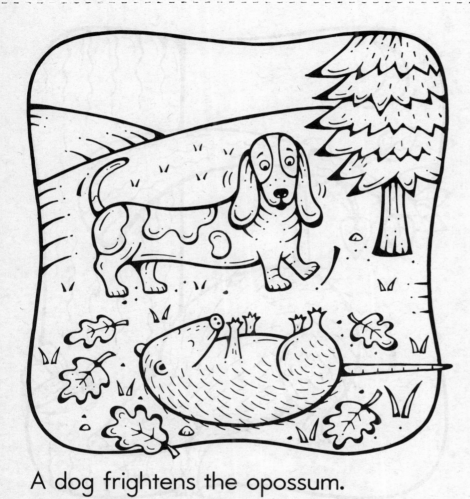

A dog frightens the opossum.
The opossum freezes. She stays still
and plays dead.
She "plays opossum."

It is light.
"Wake up! Wake up!" the birds call.
"The sun is high. The day is bright.
Wake up!"

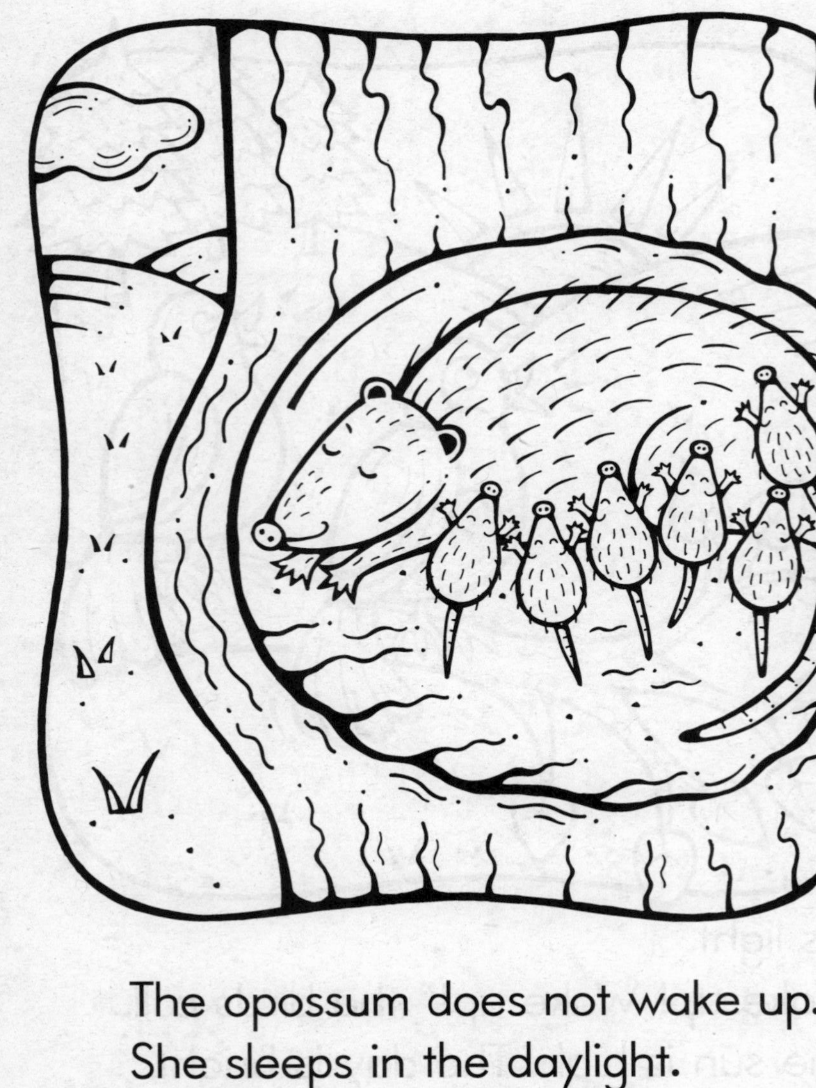

The opossum does not wake up.
She sleeps in the daylight.
Her babies hold on tight.

When it is night, she wakes up.
She hunts for insects to feed her babies.

"It is hot and dry out here," Bly says.
"I feel better in the sand.
I will stay just the way I am."

Have child read this book to you, sign here, and return ______________________

Why, Bly?

by Dottie Raymer
illustrated by Susan Nethery

MHEonline.com

Imprint 2012

Printed in the United States of America.

Send all inquiries to:
SRA/McGraw-Hill
8787 Orion Place
Columbus, OH 43240-4027

The McGraw-Hill Companies

Bly is an ostrich.
She has a small head.
She likes to stick her head into the sand.
The animals feel that Bly is an odd bird.

"Bly, why do you stick your head into the sand?" cries a child.
"Are you shy?"

"I am not shy," Bly replies.

"Bly, why do you stick your head into the sand?" cries Eagle. "Why not fly in the sky, like me?"

"I am too big to fly," replies Bly. "I like myself the way I am."

"Bly, why do you stick your head into the sand?" cries Snake. "Why not lie in the sun, like me?"

"I do not want to lie in the sun," Bly replies. "I like myself the way I am."

"Bly, why do you stick your head into the sand?" cries Chimp. "Why not climb a tree, like me?"

"I do not want to climb trees," Bly replies. "I like myself the way I am."

"Bly, why do you stick your head into the sand?" cries Lion. "Why not hunt, like me?"

"I do not want to hunt," Bly replies. "I like myself the way I am."

Have child read this book to you, sign here, and return ____________________

SRA Early Interventions in Reading

Level 1

Cranky Hank

"Well, Hank," said the farmer,
"you are a hero.
Your honking saved the day.
Every farm needs a hero, even a
cranky one!"

The police thanked Hank,
but the robber thanked the farmer!

Cranky Hank

by Robert R. O'Brien
illustrated by Elaine Garvin

Columbus, OH

The McGraw-Hill Companies

MHEonline.com

McGraw-Hill SRA

Imprint 2012

Printed in the United States of America.

Send all inquiries to:
SRA/McGraw-Hill
8787 Orion Place
Columbus, OH 43240-4027

The McGraw-Hill Companies

The police got the robber.
The farmer got Hank.

Hank kept honking and hissing.
He ran after the robber
and chased him up a lamp.

Hank was cranky.

He was always honking and hissing.
He even honked at the farmer.

A robber ran out of the bank.
He jumped into the van!
Hank's box tipped over.
Hank flapped out of the box.
Hank was very cranky!

On the way to the market,
she stopped at a bank.

In the dark, Hank stopped honking.
But if something woke Hank,
he made such a racket
that no one on the farm could sleep.

"Hank, I think it is time to sell you,"
said the farmer.
Hank honked and hissed.

The farmer put Hank in a box.
She put the box in her van.

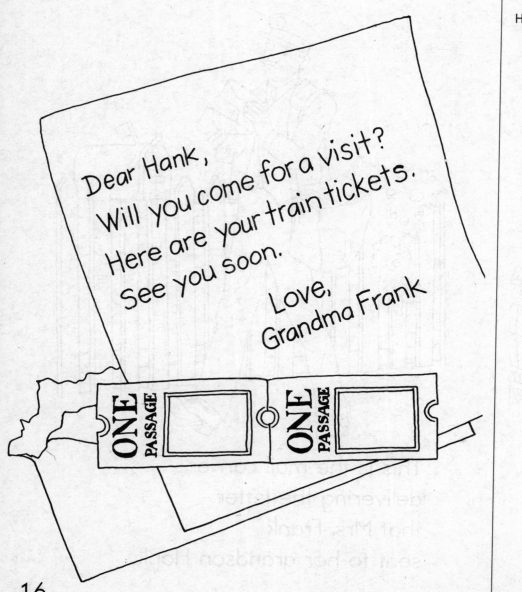

Dear Hank,
Will you come for a visit?
Here are your train tickets.
See you soon.
Love,
Grandma Frank

ONE PASSAGE
ONE PASSAGE

Have child read this book to you, sign here, and return ______________

Mail Train

by Alice Cary
illustrated by Charles Shaw

SRA
Columbus, OH
The McGraw-Hill Companies

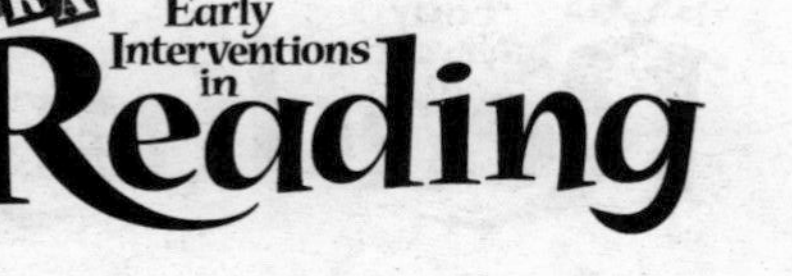

car-whacker—someone who checks trains

MHEonline.com

McGraw Hill SRA

Imprint 2012

Printed in the United States of America.

Send all inquiries to:
SRA/McGraw-Hill
8787 Orion Place
Columbus, OH 43240-4027

The McGraw-Hill Companies

This is the mail carrier
delivering the letter
that Mrs. Frank
sent to her grandson Hank.

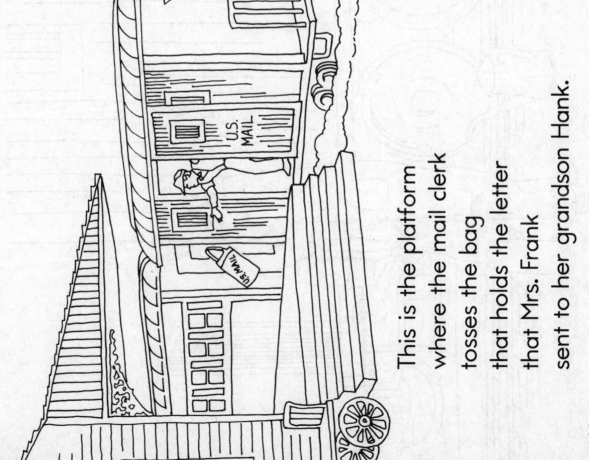

This is the platform
where the mail clerk
tosses the bag
that holds the letter
that Mrs. Frank
sent to her grandson Hank.

hotbox—a wheel part
that gets too hot

This is Mrs. Frank
sending a letter
to her grandson Hank.

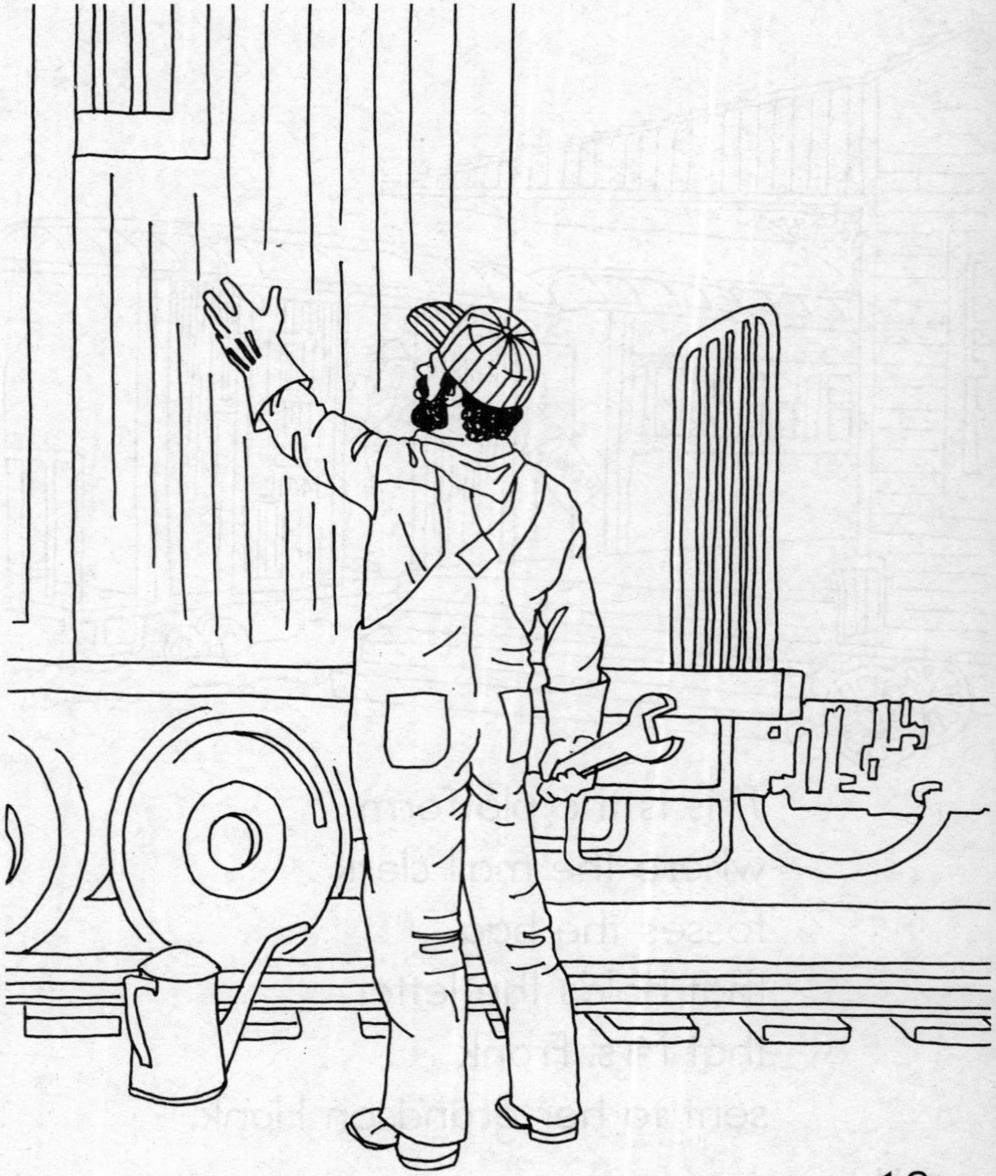

This is a car-whacker
fixing the mail car
on the train
that carries the bag
that holds the letter
that Mrs. Frank
sent to her grandson Hank.

This is the bag
that holds the letter
that Mrs. Frank
sent to her grandson Hank.

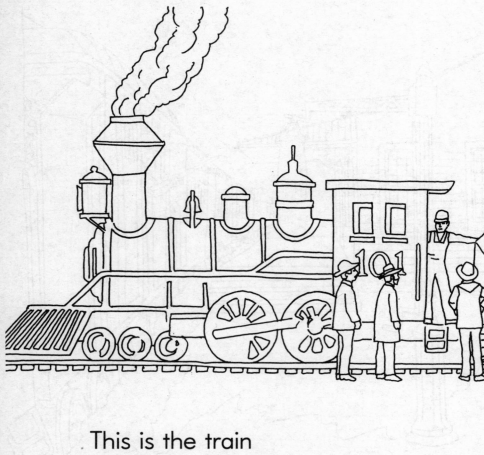

This is the train
that carries the bag
that holds the letter
that Mrs. Frank
sent to her grandson Hank.

"Stop the train!"
cries the car-whacker.
"We have a hotbox!"

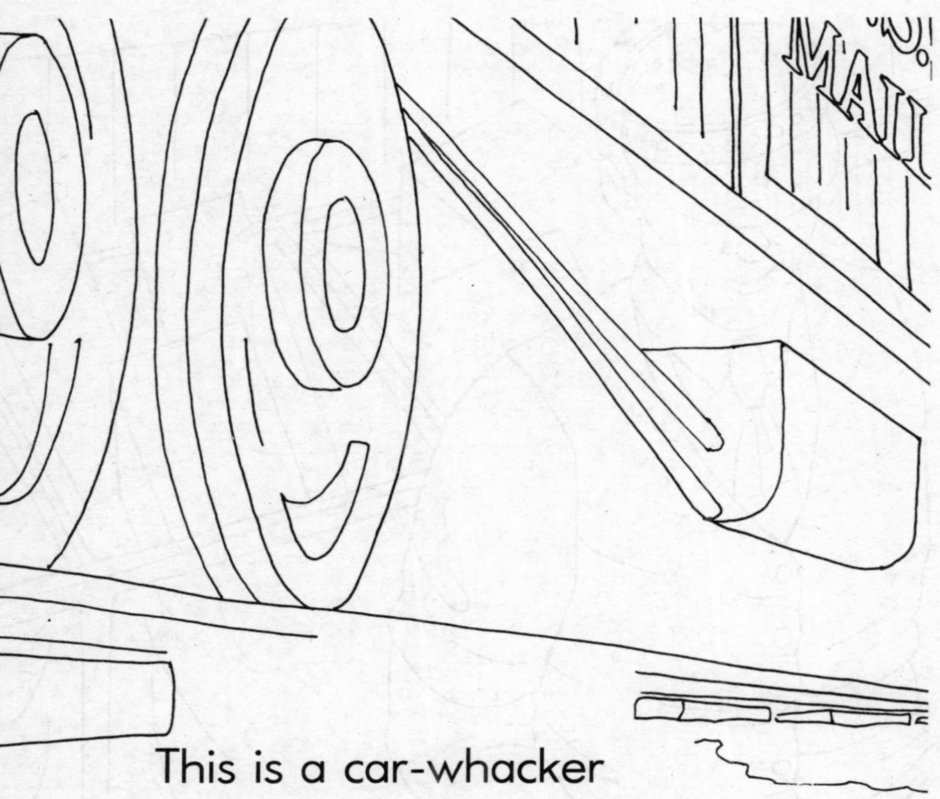

This is a car-whacker
checking the mail car
on the train
that carries the bag
that holds the letter
that Mrs. Frank
sent to her grandson Hank.

This is the mail car
on the train
that carries the bag
that holds the letter
that Mrs. Frank
sent to her grandson Hank.

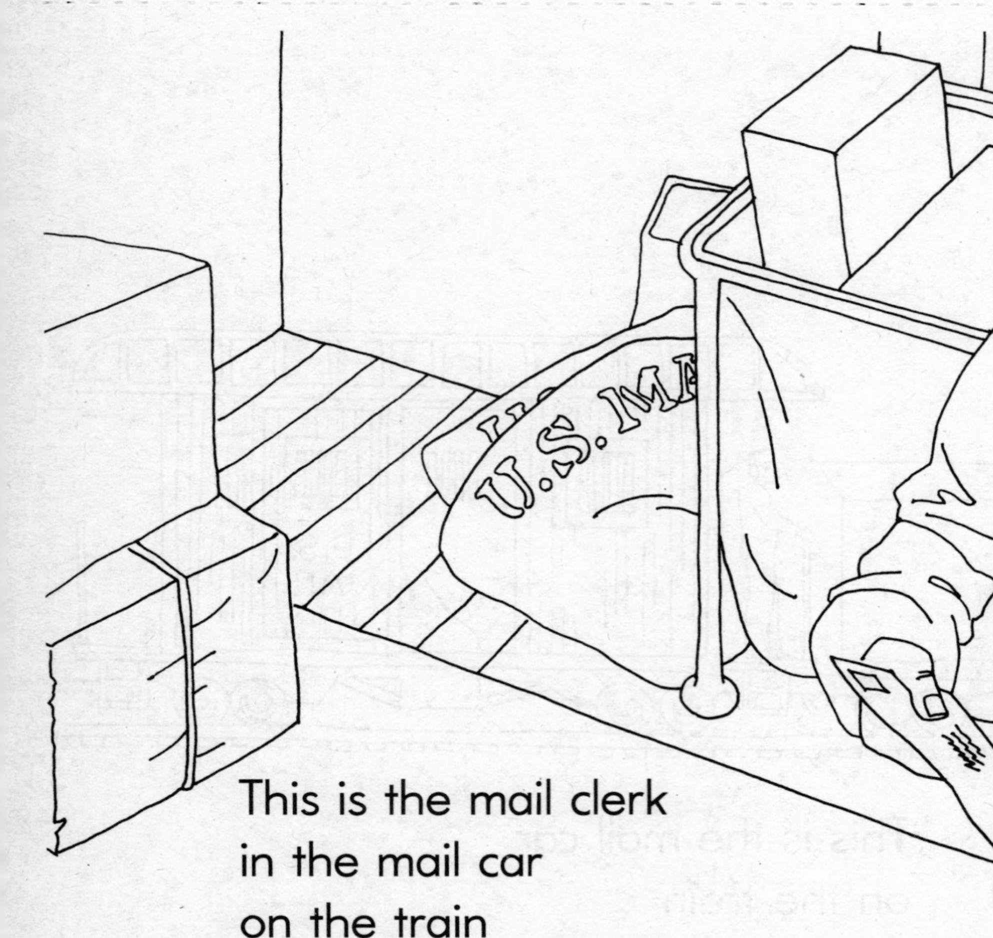

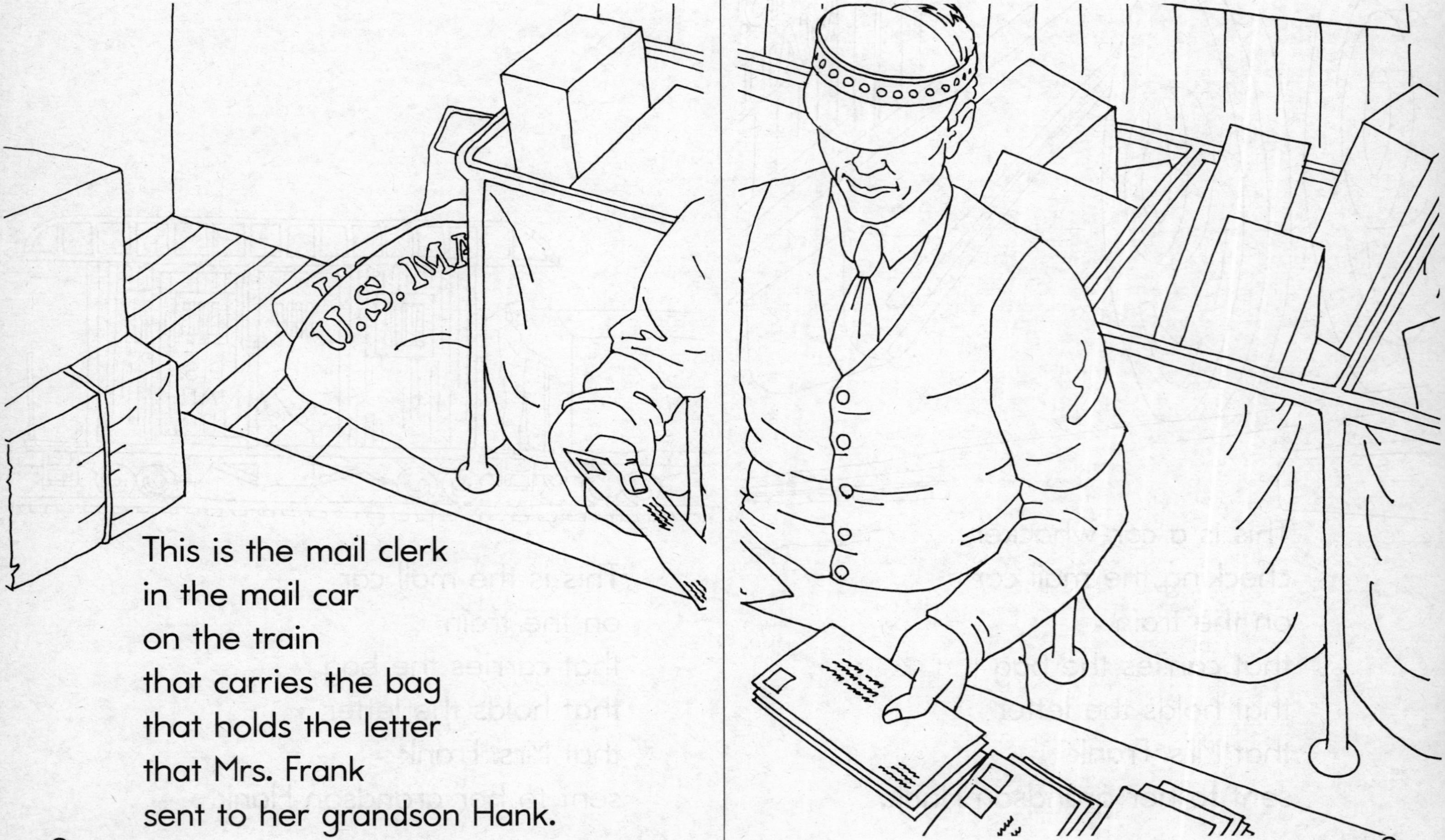

This is the mail clerk
in the mail car
on the train
that carries the bag
that holds the letter
that Mrs. Frank
sent to her grandson Hank.

And Queen Fay answered:
“You need not tell me that!
King Ray is never on time to dine!”

Have child read this book to you, sign here, and return ____________________

The King Who Was Late

by Karen Herzoff
illustrated by Anthony Accardo

Columbus, OH

The McGraw-Hill Companies

MHEonline.com

 SRA

Imprint 2012

Printed in the United States of America.

Send all inquiries to:
SRA/McGraw-Hill
8787 Orion Place
Columbus, OH 43240-4027

The McGraw-Hill Companies

Princess Paige told Queen Fay:
"King Ray may not be on time
to dine tonight."

Prince Henry told Princess Paige:
"Tell Queen Fay that King Ray
may add the right spice and
make a fine dinner tonight."

The Message

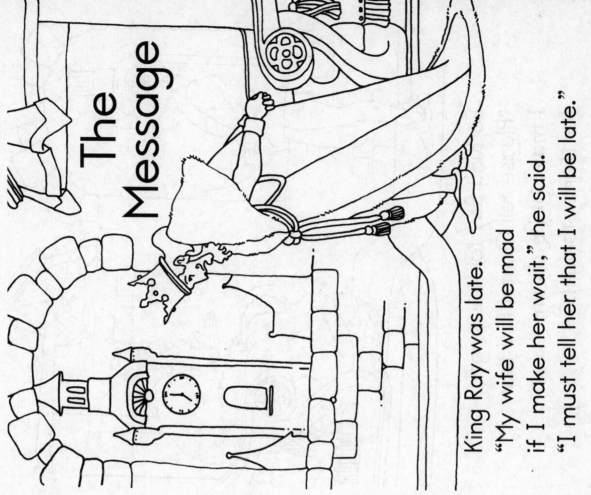

King Ray was late.
"My wife will be mad
if I make her wait," he said.
"I must tell her that I will be late."

So King Ray told his page:
"Please tell Queen Fay that
I may not be on time
for dinner tonight."

The maid told Prince Henry:
"Tell Queen Fay that
King Ray might fight thieves twice
before dinner tonight."

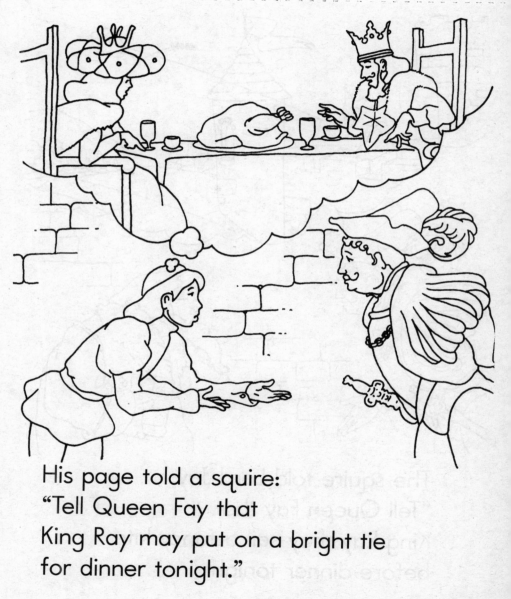

His page told a squire:
"Tell Queen Fay that
King Ray may put on a bright tie
for dinner tonight."

The squire told Lord Jay:
"Tell Queen Fay that
King Ray may sail a fancy kite
before dinner tonight."

The Answer

The duchess told a maid:
"Tell Queen Fay that
King Ray may invite five mice
to dinner tonight."

Lord Jay told a mayor:
"Tell Queen Fay that
King Ray may have a slice of pie
for dinner tonight."

The mayor told a duchess:
"Tell Queen Fay that
King Ray may need some nice rice
for dinner tonight."